And Who Shall Teach the Teachers?
The Christ Impulse in Waldorf Education

Colloquium held
in Spring Valley, New York
13 - 14 January 2005

Jointly sponsored by the

Pedagogical Section Council of North America,
Anthroposophical Society in America

and the

Teacher Education Committee
Association of Waldorf Schools
of North America

Editor: Douglas Gerwin

Pedagogical Section Council (2005)
James Pewtherer (Chair)
Douglas Gerwin
Antje Ghaznavi
Susan Howard
Ina Jaehnig
Betty Staley
Roberto Trostli
Frances Vig
Jane Wulsin

Teacher Education Committee (2005)
John Brousseau (Chair)
Douglas Gerwin
Cat Greenstreet
Diana Hughes
Scott Olmsted
Betty Staley

Table of Contents

Introduction
Douglas Gerwin

Few subjects today are more charged, and therefore more prone to misunderstanding and hurt feelings, than the role of religion or moral development in the education of youth. At one end the cry goes up for a return to fundamental values as espoused by institutionalized religion; at the other, voices of equal strength press for independence from all forms of organized religious practice in education, especially in public or state schools. In some parts of the world, for instance the Middle East, the state may actually require schools to base their curriculum on a prescribed set of religious beliefs; in other parts, most notably the United States, the state explicitly forbids any religious instruction or practice in its own schools.

Between the Skylla of mandatory school religion and the Charybdis of school religion banned outright, the debate rages over the wisdom and efficacy of religious training in education. Waldorf schools, which are open to children of all religious persuasions, often get caught in the crossfire; sometimes they are charged with being too Christian, at other times with being too pagan. For instance, I recall that some years ago a European Waldorf school was accused of practicing pagan rituals during a mid-summer ceremony in which students supposedly rode naked on horseback through the school grounds and then leapt through a huge bonfire on the sports field behind the school. In fact, the graduating seniors (fully clothed) had ridden *bareback* (without saddles) around an open bonfire during an outdoor school assembly celebrating the Christian festival of St. John. And yet for many years the charge of pagan practices lingered because the school, working out of anthroposophy and Rudolf Steiner's indications on education, was perceived as following an unorthodox spiritual path.

More common, however, is the complaint that Waldorf schools practice Christian rituals while downplaying, perhaps even denying, their Christian roots, for instance in the seasonal festivals. It does not take much research to discover that Rudolf Steiner, speaking at the assemblies of the first Waldorf school in Stuttgart, Germany, repeatedly invoked the name of Christ as the guiding spirit of the school and the "teachers' greatest Teacher". How could a Waldorf school deny its Christian character when its founder explicitly invoked the Christ as its guardian?

And yet the matter is not quite so simple or so stark. One needs, first, to enquire what Rudolf Steiner meant by "the Christ". He spoke of "the Christ Impulse" or "the Christ Event" or "the Christ-principle"; these are not the terms of orthodox Christianity, nor were they intended to be. It should be noted, further, that Steiner insisted on unqualified freedom in matters of religious practice and felt "that the only true Christianity is the Christianity which makes possible absolute freedom in the religious life."[1] In fact, he spoke of the mission of the Christ as concerning human development quite independent of any religious practice. Christ's mission "consisted in bringing to all mankind the full force of the ego, an inner independence in the soul."[2] Indeed, Steiner predicted there would come a time when Christianity as it is commonly practiced today would pass away, but the central role of the Christ in helping people become more fully human would continue:

> *Think of a remote, lonely island to which no single record of the Mystery of Golgotha has ever found its way. If human beings there through their spiritual life consciously draw the powers of earliest childhood into themselves until they reach old age, then they are Christians in the true sense of the word. In such circumstances there is no need for them to search in the Gospels, for Christianity itself is a living power and will evolve to further and further stages . . . . Times will come when Christ will be referred to in an entirely different way, when sources of an essentially different character will be in existence, when*

there will be no reference to the external history of the existence of such a Being, but when this fact will be revealed by the actual consciousness of mankind.[3]

In other words, when Rudolf Steiner invokes the Christ as the guiding spirit behind the Waldorf schools, this is not a call to Christian worship nor is it an appeal to any sectarian Christian doctrine. What is it, then?

This was the question that prompted representatives of the five major Waldorf teacher education institutes in the Association of Waldorf Schools of North America (AWSNA) to call together colleagues in the field of adult education to explore how the question of the Christ Impulse is addressed in schools and in the preparation of new teachers. The colloquium was jointly sponsored with the Pedagogical Section Council (PSC) of the Anthroposophical Society, a group of about ten Waldorf teachers who come together four times a year to examine the deeper foundations of Waldorf education.

Three of the essays in this monograph are based on presentations to that colloquium, which was held over two days in January 2005 at Sunbridge College in Chestnut Ridge, New York. The basic question addressed by this colloquium was: What does Rudolf Steiner mean by the Christ Impulse and how can one speak about it in Waldorf teacher education programs and schools without being misconstrued?

The three opening presentations addressed the theme of the colloquium from the perspectives of past, present, and future. Thereafter, the colloquium broke into several working groups, each of which included some artistic practice. Roberto Trostli, a long-standing Waldorf elementary and high school teacher and a member of the PSC, spoke first concerning the Christ Impulse in our present times. With clear and lucid examples taken from his years of classroom experience, he described how children come into the world in order to take on three crucial tasks having to do with the development of their full humanity; these tasks can be accomplished only by incarnating in flesh and bone. Teachers are there to assist the children in these tasks, he said, and the Christ stands behind the teachers in this endeavor. In other words, the Christ serves as guide to the attainment of our full humanity as individual beings working together socially with others.

Douglas Sloan, emeritus professor of education at Teachers College at Columbia University, spoke next about the historical and religious streams leading up to Christ's life on earth. Speaking out of a broad background in history and philosophy, he painted a sweeping picture of the events and the religious groups that prepared the way for the advent of the Christ. In his summation he offered five approaches to understanding what Rudolf Steiner described as "the Christ Impulse".

The theme of the future of the Christ Impulse was taken up by Betty Staley, a life-long Waldorf teacher of kindergarten through high school and also a member of the PSC. Her assignment was to explore how Waldorf teachers can work with the Christ Impulse in their own self-development as well as with their fellow human beings. This work she illustrated with living examples of her years of experience with students, with fellow teachers, and with parents at her school. She underscored the need to distinguish the Christ Impulse on one hand from the Christ Event, "an objective occurrence worthy of study and understanding", and on the other from the study of Esoteric Christianity, which goes "behind the traditional view of Christianity into deeper spiritual research."

Two further papers are included this collection. Dorit Winter, formerly a Waldorf teacher and now director of the Bay Area Center for Teacher Training, writes about the festival of Michaelmas and its direct relationship to the Christ Impulse.

Drawing from her years of careful study and annotation of Rudolf Steiner's specific curriculum indications, Dorit traces out the potent role of the Christ Impulse in each grade from first through twelfth. The other paper is an excerpt from an *amicus curiae* brief prepared by Douglas Sloan as part of a court case involving a complaint by critics of Waldorf education in the public sector that anthroposophy was a religion. In rebutting this claim, he lays out the relation of Waldorf schools to anthroposophy and its repudiation of any religious dogma. In the meantime, the case has been dismissed.

Like the colloquium itself, this collection of essays is likely to stir more questions than solutions. At the final plenum, the elusiveness of this theme became ever more apparent. Typically Rudolf Steiner places the Christ in dynamic tension *between* polar opposites – between the adversarial forces of Lucifer and Ahriman, between what was and what is to come, between the physical and the metaphysical, between the Father and the Holy Spirit, between birth in the flesh and re-birth in the spirit.

Out of one of the working groups, a poem was offered as a way of imagining this elusive and yet utterly creative betweenness wherein the Christ holds sway:

Fire

What makes a fire burn
is space between the logs,
a breathing space.
Too much of a good thing,
too many logs
packed in too tight
can douse the flames
almost as surely
as a pail of water would.

So building fires
requires attention to the spaces in between,
as much as to the wood.

When we are able to build
open spaces
in the same way
we have learned
to pile on the logs,
then we can come to see how
it is fuel, and absence of the fuel
together, that make fire possible.

We only need to lay a log
lightly from time to time.
A fire
grows
simply because the space is there,
with openings
in which the flame
that knows just how it wants to burn
can find its way.

Judy Sorum Brown[4]

References

1. Rudolf Steiner, *The Work of the Angels in Man's Astral Body* (London: Rudolf Steiner Press, 1972), p.21.
2. Rudolf Steiner, *The Gospel of St. John* (New York: Anthroposophic Press, 1962), p. 82.
3. Rudolf Steiner, *The Work of the Ego in Childhood* (Zurich, 25 February 1911, in GA 127).
4. Judy Sorum Brown, *The Sea Accepts All Rivers and Other Poems* (Miles River Press, 2000). Used by permission.

The Work of the Christ Impulse in the Work of the Waldorf Teacher

Roberto Trostli

What is the work of the Christ Impulse in our work as Waldorf teachers? I am grateful for the opportunity to address this question, but I am also humbled and daunted by this task. This is not a matter of theory but a very personal matter, for one can't address the question of the work of the Christ without coming to terms with one's own relationship to the Christ. With respect to this question, all I can offer you is my earnest striving. But if we recognize that we often learn more from those who struggle than from those who succeed, perhaps I am not entirely unsuitable to address this question.

When I look back on my work as a young Waldorf teacher, I realize that I was much more comfortable with the lecture format than I am now. Slowly I have come to realize that what needs to be said often cannot be spoken by one person alone. Two or more are needed for something greater than oneself to emerge. So I hope that you will accept my remarks merely as an introduction to our conversations and considerations, and if I stray from the path, I will trust that we will help one another find our way.

At the end of *Study of Man / Foundations of Human Experience*, Lecture 1, Rudolf Steiner says that "the human being was born. Thereby the possibility was given him to do what he could not do in the spiritual world."[1] What is not possible in the spiritual world? It is not possible to incarnate; only on earth can we "become flesh." Lofty spiritual beings watch over and guide the souls of children before they are born, but as educators we are given the privilege and responsibility of watching over and guiding a child's process of incarnation here on earth.

If we are going guide this process, we need to know something about the purpose of incarnation. Why do we become flesh? Why do we take on a material form and live in a material world? Why do we come to earth as human beings? We come to earth to develop those qualities that only human beings can develop: to learn how to love, to experience freedom, and to accept responsibility for ourselves, for others, and for the earth. Only on earth can we develop the capacities of human thinking, human feeling, and human willing. A human being who develops these capacities will be capable of fulfilling the three major challenges of human existence: to know oneself, to love one another, and to care for the earth. The capacities to meet these challenges can be learned only from other human beings. Only from others can we learn how to walk, to speak, and to think; only from them can we learn how to love and act in freedom; only from them can we learn to work together and become responsible for the earth.

Spiritual beings cannot educate us directly. They cannot help us develop capacities or intervene directly in our process of incarnation. Spiritual beings can witness, guide, and encourage us, but we ourselves have to do the heavy lifting of becoming human. These spiritual beings are intensely interested in our work, for only if we fulfill the challenging task of becoming truly human can we fulfill our role and assume responsibility for the mighty tasks of earth evolution.

In order to consider the work of the Christ Impulse in our work, we need to address the question: What is the purpose of education? We know that word "education" comes from the Latin *educare*, meaning "to bring up," or "to lead out." What do we lead out? As educators, we have the opportunity to lead out the capacities that lie in seed form in every human being. Education gives these capacities a chance to grow, to blossom, and to bear fruit.

In this way, we assist students in the process of becoming themselves, relating to others, and connecting to the world. We see how this process changes as a child develops. Young children learn to become themselves by finding a relationship to others, to the world, and finally to themselves. One could think of this as 'education from the outside in.' In adolescence and adulthood this process is transformed, and education begins to work 'from the inside out.' An adolescent first needs to develop a sense of him or herself before being able to relate to others and connect to the world.

Whatever the age, Rudolf Steiner exhorted us to view all education as a matter of self-education. The task of the teacher is therefore to provide the opportunity for the students' self-education so that they can fulfill their destinies. As teachers, we are challenged to create and develop the conditions, the activities, and the relationships through which students can become themselves.

We help young children become themselves by providing them with a human and physical environment worthy of imitation; we help elementary school children become themselves by giving them the opportunity to be disciples of adults who serve as loving authorities; and we help adolescents to become themselves by allowing them to encounter, experience, and understand the world so that they can develop their own judgment. All of this is possible only to the degree that teachers work on themselves.

In *The Child's Changing Consciousness*, Lecture 6, Rudolf Steiner speaks about the need for teachers to reach beyond their narrow selves in service of their students:

> *For people in general there may be many kinds of prayer. Over and above these there is this special prayer for the teacher: "Dear God, make that I, as far as my personal ambitions are concerned, quite obliterate*

*myself. And Christ make true in me the Pauline word, 'Not I, but the
Christ in me' . . . that the Holy Spirit may hold sway in the teacher.'*[2]

Why does a teacher need this particular prayer? What does
this prayer mean? Time allows me to share only a few thoughts.
When we say, "Dear God, make it that I, as far as my personal
ambitions are concerned, quite obliterate myself", we are asking
God for the gift of *wisdom* to help know ourselves. When we say,
"And Christ make true in me the Pauline word, 'Not I, but the
Christ in me'", we are asking the Being who embodies the power
of love for the gift of *courage* to learn how to love one another. And
when we say, "that the Holy Spirit may hold sway in the teacher",
we are asking the Holy Spirit for the gift of *strength* to become
stewards of the earth. In this threefold appeal to the trinity, we ask
for the strength, courage, and wisdom to become truly human, so
that we can fulfill our role as beings of the tenth hierarchy, who
work on behalf of our students, on behalf of humanity, and on
behalf of the earth.

If the task of the teacher is to provide the student with the
opportunities and conditions for self-education, the task of
colleagues is to provide each other with the opportunities and
conditions for each other's self-education. Colleagues provide a
mirror—an objective and, one would hope, a loving and forgiving
mirror—to help each other to become.

In my experience, parents have three questions of their
children's teachers: Do you love my child? Do you understand my
child? Do you believe in my child? I think that we have the same
three questions for one another as colleagues: Do you believe in
me? Do you understand me? Do you love me?

It is easy to bandy the word love around as if it were a gift or
a form of grace, but love is hard work. A wise man said: "Work is
love made visible," but we could also say: "Love is work made

visible." Through the hard work of interest, recognition, understanding, acceptance, support, and trust—in other words, through the hard work of love—a group of colleagues can create a community that lives in the soul of each of its members, a community that recognizes and values the virtue of each of its members.

The perception and recognition of each other's virtue is built on the foundation of a different kind of experience of one another—an experience that is so spiritualized that we enter the spiritual world and allow spiritual beings to participate in our work. Rudolf Steiner called this experience "the reverse ritual." The reverse ritual allows the power of love to manifest in our encounters so that they are transformed into sacraments that nourish spiritual beings as well as ourselves.

As colleagues, we provide each other with the opportunity for our own self-education as teachers. The teacher's teacher provides us with the opportunity for our self-education as a community of teachers. Rudolf Steiner spoke explicitly about "the teachers' Teacher" and our need to love Him. At an assembly in the first Waldorf school, he said to the students:

> *What your teachers say to you comes from incredibly hard work on their part, from the strength of their devotion and from their love for you. But what comes from their love must also be able to get to you, and that is why I always say the same thing to you: Love your teachers, because love will carry what comes from your teachers' hearts into your hearts and into your heads. Love is the best way for what teachers have to give to flow into their students. That is why I am going to ask you again today, "Do you love your teachers? Do you still love them?" [The children shout, "Yes!"]*

A little later in this assembly, Rudolf Steiner said:

> *Thus the spirit of Christ is always with you....This spirit of Christ
> is also your teachers' great teacher. Through your teachers, the spirit of
> Christ works into your hearts.*

And on another occasion he spoke directly to the teachers:

> *Dear students of the highest grade of all—that is, dear teachers! In
> this new school year, let us begin teaching with courage and enthusiasm
> to prepare these children for the school of life. Thus may the school be
> guided by the greatest leader of all, by the Christ Himself. May this be
> the case in our school.*[3]

What does our Teacher want us to learn? If all education is a
matter of self-education, the major lesson our community of
teachers has to learn from the Christ is how to become a truly
human community—a community that is built on the strength of
individual ego-hood, a community that is built on the courage of
giving and the even greater courage of receiving what others have
to give, a community that is built on the wisdom that allows us to
recognize and embrace our task.

As individuals, we are inherently one-sided and narrow, no
matter how hard we work to develop ourselves. We need one
another to create a vessel that can receive spiritual substance. We
need to learn how to transform our 'I' gesture into an 'O' gesture,
for it is in the space between and among us that something can
enter.

Where do we experience the Christ Impulse in our work as
Waldorf teachers? Where two or three are gathered in His name.
Then we form our chalice of community, asking the Christ to help
us become greater than the sum of our parts, asking Him to teach
us to transform our everyday encounters into sacraments in which
we can then experience each other's divinity, asking Him to inspire
us, to make love visible so that we can help the earth fulfill its
destiny: to become the planet of love.

References

1. Rudolf Steiner, *Study of Man* (London: Rudolf Steiner Press, 1966), p. 24.
2. Rudolf Steiner, *The Child's Changing Consciousness and Waldorf Education* (Hudson, NY: Anthroposophic Press, 1988), pp. 145-146.
3. Rudolf Steiner, *Rudolf Steiner in the Waldorf School: Lectures and Addresses to Children, Parents, and Teachers* (Hudson, NY: Anthroposophic Press, 1996), p. 210.

Toward Understanding the Christ and the Christ Impulse

Douglas Sloan

Rudolf Steiner frequently spoke of the being of Christ and of the working of what he called the Christ Impulse in human history. This is a brief attempt to identify and pull together some main considerations important to a better understanding of the Christ and the Christ Impulse. From the schematic nature of these observations, it will be obvious that they are intended as a kind of outline for further thought and research. The work of Rudolf Steiner is central to these considerations, as well as others who have themselves drawn upon Steiner.[1]

I. The Spiritual Pre-History of the Incarnation and Mystery of Golgotha[2]

Rudolf Steiner points out that the Christ has accompanied and worked for the human being from the beginning of earth existence, both as the Creator Logos and in the form of the great Sun Being who performed three crucial deeds on behalf of humankind in primordial times—in Steiner's terminology, in the Lemurian and Atlantean epochs.

Beginning with what has been termed in the Christian tradition as the Fall, and described in the Hebrew book of Genesis as the temptation in the Garden of Eden, Lucifer, and subsequently Ahriman, had begun to attack the human being with the aim of derailing human evolution and capturing the human being for themselves. In order to prevent a total subversion of human evolution by these adversarial powers, the spiritual world intervened to hold back and protect a portion of the original, androgynous Adam soul. As Lucifer's original attack was on the human astral body, a portion of the original Adam etheric body was kept back in the spiritual world, pure and undefiled, to prevent its being infected by Lucifer.

Various spiritual traditions appear to have mythological accounts reflecting this preservation and protection of the pure Adam soul. Certainly the Genesis account of the Tree of Knowledge and the Tree of Life can be seen as a vivid imagination of this event. In the Genesis story, Adam and Eve at the time of the temptation are given access to the Tree of Knowledge of good and Evil, but the Tree of Life is taken from them and access to it is denied them. A portion of the life body, the etheric body, of Adam is held back in the spiritual world, protected from the adversarial onslaught and the temptations of the human being. This pure Adam soul, this etheric Adam being, however, was not inactive. In fact, from the beginning of human evolution on earth, this Adam soul was receptive to the Christ Being, the Logos. Long before the actual incarnation of the Logos, the Christ, in the man Jesus, the pure Adam soul and the Christ Being together had worked to enable the human being to maintain and develop its uniquely human nature in spite of the attacks of the adversarial spirits.

These crucial deeds for the human being were performed by the Christ working with the pure Adam being. Early in the Lemurian age, Lucifer and Ahriman had continued their onslaught on the human being, and had caused a disruption of the human senses. This attack on the senses brought the human being under the influence of earth forces that threatened to pull the human being down and keep the human in the horizontal position of the animals. The Christ Being joining with the Adam soul, which assumed the form of an archangel, reordered the human senses, and gave the human being the capacity to lift out of the horizontal and to stand upright. Only as an erect, upright being could the human receive the uniquely Human I, the Ego, the gift of the Spirits of Form (the Exousiai, or, in Genesis, the Elohim).

This deed of the Christ-permeated Adam soul lives on and is recapitulated in the life of every human being, when as a young child the individual raises itself from the horizontal and learns to stand and walk.

This was not, however, the end of this primordial Luciferic and Ahrimanic onslaught, and in the middle of the Atlantean age these adversaries strove to disrupt the proper functioning of the human vital organs. Their effort was to render the human vital organs incapable of relating correctly with the outside world, to make these organs, in Steiner's vivid phrase, "selfish." The result was that human speech, with the turning inward of the human organs, was threatened with becoming purely subjective, capable only of subjective, animal-like emotional outbursts—cries of pain, joy, meaningless babbling. Again the Christ-permeated Adamic archangelic being intervened to reorder the organs and to give to human speech the possibility to express objective reality.

By the end of the Atlantean age, however, Lucifer and Ahriman were continuing their attack on the human being by disrupting and disordering the basic human soul functions of thinking, feeling, and willing. This disorder was reflected again in a threat to human speech, that it would never be able to grasp and express meaning. Once again, the Christ-permeated Adamic archangel intervened to reorder human speech in order that it could be uniquely human, that is, that it would be capable of grasping and expressing meaning—meaning in the world and meaning in the human soul.

Rudolf Steiner has commented that today a child learns to speak but can do so only because of these last two Christ deeds— the one to give to human speech the capacity to be objective and the other to give the capacity to grasp and express meaning. Rudolf Steiner writes: "We can enrich anew our inner feelings if we remember, when we see a child beginning to speak and gradually improving his power of expression, that the Christ-Impulse rules within the unconscious nature and that the Christ-Force lives in the child's power of speech, guarding and stimulating it."

A fourth deed, a deed of sacrifice, was the Incarnation itself and the ensuing Mystery of Golgotha, involving once more a coming together of the Christ Being, the pure Adam soul (the Tree of Life), and, also, an advanced human being of great wisdom (Zarathustra, representing the Tree of Knowledge).

II. Historical Background of the Incarnation and Mystery of Golgotha

Steiner makes clear, as no others have, how all the great, archetypal streams of spiritual wisdom converged around the origins of Christianity, coming together and joining in the Incarnation and Mystery of Golgotha. Two dimensions of this convergence need to be kept firmly in mind as the undergirding background for understanding it. Both come to full experience in the Christ event. One of these is the evolution of consciousness in human history; the other is the joining of outer- and inner-directed archetypal streams of human spiritual paths.

The first, the evolution of consciousness, has been described, not only by Steiner but by others as well, as beginning in primordial times from an original state of oneness and unity with the cosmos, a state of consciousness described by Owen Barfield as "original participation." In this state of original participation in the cosmic consciousness the human being was filled, indeed, merged with, the wisdom and life of the universe, but was so immersed in this universal consciousness as to have no sense of individual identity and self. Gradually, over long periods of time, this primal experience of oneness, of participation in a larger cosmic consciousness, began to give way to an increasing sense of separation from the whole, and to a growing sense of individual self-consciousness and self-identity. It can be shown that historically this fading of original participation could be experienced in two different ways. One way of experiencing it was as a deep sense of loss, a loss of the divine ground, a loss of the gods and of a world of nature alive with the gods, filled with spirit and meaning. The other way of experiencing the separation from original participation in cosmic consciousness was as a growing sense of inwardness, as a building up of an identity within, a sense of individual self-identity and new possibilities for individual worth and freedom. Both experiences of the evolution of consciousness figure in the historical background of the Incarnation.

The other background aspect for understanding the significance of the Incarnation is the convergence in it of the two great archetypal expressions of human spiritual streams (and of various specific forms within them): the outer- and inner-directed. The inner-directed, which had its home especially in the East, in Asia, and in India particularly, stressed the attainment of inner soul development, of inner peace, tranquility and purity. This stream reached its culmination in the life and teachings of the Buddha. The outer-directed stream was primarily associated with western and northern parts of the ancient world: Persia, the lands of the Celts and Germanic tribes, and Judaism. This stream found one of its great expressions in the ancient Zarathustra of Persia, who in his awareness of the Being of Light, Ahura Mazdao, and the Being of Darkness, Ahriman, saw the essential spiritual task as one of grappling with the powers of good and evil in the world itself.

Both of these archetypal streams came together in the Incarnation of the Christ. In fact, Rudolf Steiner points out how all of the archetypal spiritual streams came to early awareness of the great Sun Being, the Christ, approaching the earth. In India, this being was known as Vishva Karma; in Iran as Ahura Mazdao; in Egypt as Osiris; in Greece as Apollo; in Judaism as reflected in Yahweh. The convergence of the archetypal pre-Christian spiritual streams in the Christ event can be seen in the coming together of the ancient mysteries, Judaism, the Essenes, Gnosticism, Iranian Zoroastrianism, and Buddhism. All converge in the Christ event and in doing so reflect in various ways the play of the evolution of consciousness and the joining of the inner and outer spiritual orientations.

1. The Mysteries

The rise in the late nineteenth century of scholarship in comparative religion and of historical criticism of scriptural texts posed a fundamental challenge to traditional Christianity. Many scholars in these fields began to detect a deep similarity between Christianity and the ancient mystery religions with their various emphases on dying and rising gods (such as in the myths of Persephone and Demeter, or of Isis and Osiris). There was a strong tendency among many of these scholars to reject Christianity as being just another, more recent mystery cult, and to regard the mystery cults themselves, and their myths, as essentially human projections. This meant for these scholars the elimination of any cosmic dimension for an understanding of the Christ, and left for many of them only two options: either to abandon Christianity, or to interpret it as essentially the teachings and example of Jesus, "the simple man of Nazareth."

Rudolf Steiner was one of the few at the time, at the end of the nineteenth century, to meet this challenge head on. In his lectures, published in 1904 under the title *Christianity as Mystical Fact*, Steiner maintained with careful argument that the Christ event was, indeed, deeply related to the ancient Mysteries. The Christ event—the Incarnation and the Mystery of Golgotha—was, he argued, an enactment in history of the cosmic significance of the Mysteries. Although it involves here a drastic over-simplification of Steiner's treatment in *Christianity as Mystical Fact*, perhaps we can gain some sense of the deep significance that he saw in the Mysteries for understanding the Christ event.

Much remains unknown about the Mysteries, owing especially to the fact that revealing the inner secrets of the Mysteries carried with it in ancient times the penalty of death. Nevertheless, certain essential knowledge about them has come down to us. There were in ancient time many Mystery Centers and versions of the

Mysteries. All, however, seem to have had certain elements in common. First, all possessed a sense of the cosmic origins of all things. They saw and experienced the world as an emanation of the divine source of the universal all. And these cosmic realities as they experienced them were captured, expressed, and transmitted in mythological form, as great story pictures. The myths varied from people to people, but all shared a similar sense of the cosmic origins of the world. Also common to the Mysteries was an emphasis on space. The spatial world—and usually it was the very defined world of the particular people—was seen and experienced as the microcosm of the macrocosm. Space and nature were experienced as suffused with divine beings and with divine energies and forces. From this perspective, time was of secondary importance to space, for time was experienced as cyclical, endlessly repeating itself in the seasons and regularities of nature in a perpetual dying and renewal of the earth. The myths and rituals of the mysteries reenacted and made possible the participation of the people in the earth's timeless relationship with the spiritual cosmos.

Also common to the Mysteries was a real sense of the Fall from original participation. Yet the experience of this separation within the Mysteries was not so extreme that a reconnection with the spiritual world—at least for certain persons—was impossible. Rites of initiation, usually rigorous and grueling, enabled selected individuals to experience the spiritual world and to return from that experience with renewed, or newly acquired, authority and wisdom. These initiates also became witness to the promise of immortality. Initiation was only for the few, chiefly for the priest-king. The masses, the people, honored the priest-king as their divinely imbued leader and carrier of their sense of identity. The priest-king provided the sense of I for the group soul of his people. A few other select persons also underwent initiation, and these were often revered as the main guardians of wisdom and a prime source of revelation for human beings from the spiritual world.

The myths of many ancient people attribute the origins of major human cultural advances—agriculture, the taming of animals, the discovery of pottery and weaving, and so forth—to divine revelations bestowed upon leading initiates of the Mysteries.

It was the cosmic, spiritual consciousness and connection suffusing the Mysteries which was then brought into and enacted in history in the Christ event.

2. Judaism

The emergence of the Jewish people was a first herald, and special representation, of a new stage in the evolution of consciousness. A number of characteristics set the Jewish people distinctly apart from the world of the Mysteries out of which they emerged. Three of these differences are especially important here.

a) A growing sense of inwardness. The Jewish scriptures witness to the emergence among the Jewish people of a gradually developing I consciousness. In the burning bush, the God of the Jews announces itself to Moses as "I Am the I Am." The prophet discovers God not in the world, not in the storm, not in the wind and lightning, but in the "still, small voice within." An emerging sense of individuality, of I-ness, was at once a prerequisite for, and also a result of, being spoken to by the divine experience as I Am. The new monotheism of the Jews was itself the expression of a new sense of an inwardly integrated oneness of Self. The Jewish people still experienced themselves in a group soul whose I was carried by the Fathers—Abraham, Isaac, and Jacob. But a developing sense of individuality was emerging, encouraged by the prophets who were themselves addressed by God as individuals and who called the people to their moral responsibility before God and their duty to fulfill the God-given Law. In this sense, the Jewish Law can be seen as a kind of schoolmaster, an essential schoolmaster, for the development of a sense of increasing individual identity—of a self that can be held accountable before the Law.

b) A new sense of history. A new sense of the reality of history set the Jewish people off radically from the Mysteries. For the Mysteries, time was experienced as essentially cyclical, endlessly repeating itself. The Jewish people were among the first, if not the first, to experience the uniqueness of events in time. Time was experienced by them not as cyclical, but flowing, as it were, in a straight line, with each event happening but once and, therefore, loaded with potential moral significance. The uniqueness of events in time made time, not space, the prime medium for both divine and human action. Time acquired for the Jewish people a heightened meaning and moral significance.

c) Creation. For the Jewish people the world was experienced as God's creation. The world for the Jews was not, as it was for the earlier Mysteries, a divine emanation still charged with divine beings and spiritual energies. The world for the Jews was in a real sense "a finished work." Space, for the Jews, was, accordingly, as it was not for the Mysteries, drained of divinity. The world was God's creation and a place in which moral responsibility in time could be worked out. Such a view of the world offered new moral possibilities and an arena for pursuing these. But such a world could also be experienced as an alien and lonely place. Many of the Jewish people were not immune to the temptation to return to the reassuring presence of the nature gods worshipped by the surrounding peoples. The ferocity with which the prophet Elijah, for example, smote the priests of Baal is evidence of the lingering presence of this temptation, and the need to combat it. The view of the world as a divine creation, however, even as a finished product, enabled the Jewish people to establish a new relationship to the divine, to the world, and to themselves—a relationship radically different from that of the Mysteries.

Did Judaism, then, as Andrew Welburn asks, break entirely with the Mysteries? "The answer is no."

3. The Essenes

Very early in the twentieth century, Rudolf Steiner pointed, and in some detail, to the importance of a religious movement within Judaism known as the Essenes, a movement that appeared in Judaism just a couple of centuries before the birth of Christ. Steiner was very much alone in emphasizing the importance of the Essenes, since little was known of them, and most scholars dismissed them as a relatively insignificant group. This changed suddenly after World War II with the discovery of the Dead Sea Scrolls, which provided detailed evidence of the presence and importance of the Essenes and their communities just before and at the time of Jesus. Today scholars seem to agree that there were three major parties within Judaism at the time of Jesus: the Sadducees, the aristocratic priestly caste; the Pharisees, the representatives of rabbinic Judaism; and the Essenes.

Steiner also very early on pointed to something else about the Essenes that scholars have only relatively recently begun to recognize. There was, on the one hand, central to the Essenes a heightened emphasis on stringent obedience to the Jewish Law. However, there was also, on the other hand, something else: namely, the influence of esoteric sects that practiced baptismal, initiatory rites—in other words, mystery rites and practices. And, of special significance, many of these mystery practices within the Essenes could be traced back and linked to the spiritual world of Iran, particularly to the tradition of Zarathustra.

As Welburn says, the Essenes constituted a coming together, a remarkable fusion, of spiritual realities and outlooks that previously had existed apart and in many respects in contradiction to one another: the Mysteries, with their cosmic consciousness and baptismal rites of initiation, and, at the same time, the Jewish feeling for history, for responsibility toward the earth, and for moral responsibility before the Law. As Welburn also makes clear, however, there was a certain weakness in the Essene outlook and practice. Humans were still to measure themselves against an external yardstick, the Law, and righteousness was for the few. True righteousness could be attained only by those who joined the Essene community and followed its rules of strict obedience. As Welburn says, this entailed righteousness for the few, but guilt for the many.

In his lectures on *The Fifth Gospel*, Rudolf Steiner describes the inner suffering experienced by the young Jesus of Nazareth at his awareness of this. Jesus and John the Baptist, Steiner says, were not members of the Essenes but were intimately acquainted with them. Steiner describes Jesus' experience of how the adversarial spirits of Lucifer and Ahriman halted outside the gates of the Essene communities and instead of trying to enter in to subvert them, turned to spread fear and guilt throughout the wider world beyond. Jesus, rather than joining the elite, righteous few, instead turned to the world at large, and, as Welburn says, thus made the Mystery of the few available to all humankind.

Complicating the picture so far is the fact that the Jewish worldview, in general and as heightened in the Essenes, posed a fundamental problem—an insurmountable obstacle—for many people in the Near East and Orient. There were two sides to the problem. The Jewish experience of an intensified self-consciousness, an experience becoming more and more widespread beyond Judaism, was felt by many people as alienation from the divine. A growing sense of individuality was felt by many people not, as it was for the Jews, as a call for moral responsibility before the Law, but as separation from God, as a loss of the gods. And, added to this, the Jewish view of creation as a "finished work" was experienced increasingly by many people as a loss of the divine presence in the world. The material world was for many, indeed, a lonely and meaningless place, and a place of incredible suffering and hardship. And for many, many people at the time, this was undoubtedly a quite realistic assessment.

The Jewish worldview led for many to a reaction in the form of the Gnostics.

4. Gnosticism

Gnosticism represented a return to the archaic view of the ancient Mysteries, but with a difference. The Gnostics, like others at the time besides the Jews, were experiencing humanity's increasingly pronounced loss of connection with the spiritual world. Consequently, they were predisposed to accept the Jewish view of the world as a created, finished product. But, unlike the Jews, they experienced this world as a frightening, terrible world, lonely and full of suffering. They saw this world as a created world, but one created by a lesser god, a god they called the Demiurge, and whom they identified with the god of the Old Testament. This god of the Old Testament, this Demiurge, they saw as, at best, a bumbling, if not an out and out malevolent, divinity who had created a world of matter, arid and void of spirit.

There were many Gnostic systems: Pagan Gnostics, Samaritan Gnostics, Greek Gnostics, and, for a couple of centuries, Christian Gnostics. The Christian Church fairly early rejected Gnosticism and nearly succeeded in wiping out the writings of its representatives to such an extent that for centuries all that could be known of them was descended from the hands of their Church opponents. With the discovery of the Gnostic manuscripts at Nag Hammadi in 1945, however, it soon became evident that the Gnostics were much more influential in early Christianity than had until then been supposed. Many of Rudolf Steiner's earlier statements about the nature and importance of the Gnostics acquired historical confirmation through the discovery at Nag Hammadi.

The systems of the various forms of Gnosticism all involved incredibly complex pictures of the spiritual world. The teachings of Valentinus, an early, influential Christian Gnostic, for example, present a picture of the spiritual world that ranged from the Supreme Father, unbegotten and dwelling alone and beyond the universe, through more than thirty levels of lesser, but still very high, beings who existed as emanations of the high godhead, all the way down to a fallen aspect of Sophia, who was herself the creator both of matter, and, finally, of the Demiurge, the Old Testament god, who then created this world out of *mater, psyche,* and *pneuma.* The various systems all, however, had a common, core account of the world. They all held the view that human beings were once merged and united with the high godhead. Owing to a kind of primordial catastrophe, humans were scattered in the world of matter of the Demiurge as illusory selves. Most of the humans living in this world, nevertheless, possessed deep within them a hidden spark of the godhead. The task of salvation was to identify this spark and ascend to merge once more with the godhead. This task of salvation consisted of two steps: First, it was necessary to know the situation. True knowledge (*Gnosis*—the Greek word for knowledge) of the nature of the world and of the human plight was required. Second, to escape entrapment in the world of matter, it was necessary through gnosis and initiatory rites, to dissolve the illusory, earthy individual. Thus the primal reality of unity— of merger—with the high Godhead, could be restored.

As noted, Steiner pointed out that Gnosticism was very influential in early Christianity, as has been confirmed by such Nag Hammadi documents as *The Gospel of Thomas.* And New Testament scholars have detected a Gnostic style and mode of thinking present in such Gospels as those of Mark and John. Steiner, at points, has offered a high estimation of the Gnostics, even though he says the Church was right in eventually rejecting them. There were three main reasons for the Church's rejection of Gnosticism: 1) the Gnostics' dualism between matter (evil) and the spirit (good); 2) their view of the unreality of the self; and 3) what is called their docetism, from the Greek word meaning "to appear" or "to seem." For the Gnostics it was an outrage to suggest that a high spiritual being like the Christ would incarnate in evil matter and then, worse, suffer an ignominious execution as a common criminal. The crucifixion of Christ, they argued, therefore was only an appearance; it was docetic, he only seemed to be crucified. With respect to this docetic element, the Gospels of Mark and John are very interesting in that, as Welburn shows, they contain Gnostic elements in their descriptions of the cosmic Christ entering the man Jesus, but then turn Gnosticism against itself by affirming unequivocally both the real crucifixion and death of Jesus and the value of the individual, of history, and of earth existence.

Steiner says that the Church was ultimately right in rejecting Gnosticism, but that it overreacted in doing so. The Gnostics possessed a cosmic consciousness that enabled them to recognize the cosmic Christ in the man Jesus. When this consciousness faded, the Church's doctrines affirming the cosmic dimension of Christ Jesus tended to become increasingly formal and abstract, and more and more inaccessible as living experience. The Gnostics spoke of a divine cosmic process in which the human is involved. As Welburn comments, when this cosmic dimension becomes incorporated into history it acquires a significance the Gnostics themselves could not give it. This joining of the cosmic and the historical is precisely what Rudolf Steiner explores in *Christianity as Mystical Fact.*

5. Buffddhism

More is said below about the involvement of Buddhism in the Christ event. Suffice it here simply to note that Buddhist influences were present in the Near East already during very early Christian times. Alexander the Great (356-323 B.C.) subdued Greece, Egypt, Persia, and India, thus opening the Orient, which then poured back into Greece and Palestine.

By the time of Christianity, we can see that many spiritual streams were converging: the individual moral and historical consciousness of Judaism; the rationalism of Greece (which we only note here); the return of the ancient Mysteries—the primal spirituality of Egypt, Iran, and Greece—to Judaism in the Essenes and Gnostics; the continuation of the Iranian tradition of Zarathustra; and Buddhist influences. Against this background, Rudolf Steiner's description of how the Christ event was an incorporation of the convergence of these great, archetypal spiritual streams of humankind acquires all the more force and significance.

III. The Incarnation

1. The Immediate Background

The births of the Jesus child as depicted in the Gospels of Matthew and Luke respectively present two radically different images of the expected Messiah, and are clearly accounts of two different births. The differences between the two are many and profound, a fact almost totally lost in traditional Christianity. For the sake of brevity we note only one difference here. The Gospel of Matthew describes the coming of a Kingly Messiah, tracing the genealogy of Jesus through Abraham to David and one of David's sons, Solomon. Luke, however, describes the birth of a different Messiah, essentially a priestly Messiah, tracing the genealogy of Jesus back to Nathan, another son of David, and from Nathan back to Adam and from Adam to God. (For shorthand purposes, the one Jesus can be referred to as the Solomon Jesus, the other as the Nathan Jesus.)

Of great interest is that the Essenes had both traditions. They expected two Messiahs, not one. They expected a high priestly Messiah, the Messiah of Aaron, and a kingly Messiah from Judah, the Messiah of Israel. In their expectation of the Kingly Messiah, the Essenes held to the traditional Iranian prophecy of twelve reincarnations of the great leader Zarathustra, and a thirteenth reincarnation of him in which he was to be the vessel of some great being. In the Gospel of Matthew "Magi" appear at the birth of Jesus. A magus was a priest of Iranian Zoroastrianism. The presence of the Magi in Matthew points to the fact that Christianity came not only as a fulfillment of the hopes of Judaism for the Messiah, but also as fulfilling the prophecies of ancient Iran, a reborn Zarathustra.

Before the discovery of the Dead Sea Scrolls, the only clear indication of this double Messianic expectation was in the lectures and writings of Rudolf Steiner. Now, moreover, in the documents of the Essenes that have been discovered, there is also suggested, as Welburn points out, a secret Essene line of teaching which held that the unity of the Kingly and the Priestly would be accomplished in the last incarnation of the Zoroastrian savior, Zarathustra. As Welburn observes: "It is fascinating to read Rudolf Steiner's description of how the twin ideals came together, as a matter of historical occurrence, in the development of Jesus of Nazareth from his childhood to the point where he accepted the astonishing responsibility of his mission. His [Steiner's] account has only gained in force and relevance with the modern discoveries which have confirmed so much of what he had to say."

2. The Two Jesus Children

According to Rudolf Steiner, the infancy story in the Gospel of Matthew describes the reincarnation of the great spiritual leader, Zarathustra, in whom was incorporated through his many repeated lives on earth a wisdom of unparalleled depth. The infancy story in Luke, Steiner says, describes the incarnation, for the first time, of the pure Adam soul, that portion of the etheric body of the original androgynous Adam held back in the spiritual world so that it would be protected from Lucifer. This was the Adam soul that we have already seen joining with the Christ on behalf of the human being in primordial times. This is the pure, undefiled Adam soul that is born for the first time in the Nathan Jesus child of the Gospel of Luke.

According to Steiner, Gautama the Buddha was active and associated with the birth of the Nathan Jesus. From the heavenly heights, Steiner says, the Buddha sent his Nirmanakaya body to hover over the child. In Buddhist doctrine there are three Buddha bodies, the lowest of which is the Nirmanakaya body associated with the physical body of the historical Gautama Buddha. This body, however, has peculiar characteristics, signified in the names by which it is also known in Buddhist doctrine: "the body of appearance" and "the body of transformation," among others. This is the body by which Gautama can manifest to human beings as the physical Gautama, but, like a similar body in one form of Gnosticism, it is an "appearance body," a "body of transformation": it can also manifest in non-human forms. And it can manifest as "the vehicle of glory" in heavenly displays; it can "cause," as one scholar of Buddhism puts it, "a super-human image, perceptible yet not material to appear in Paradise." This accords very well with Steiner's description of the appearance to the shepherds in the Gospel of Luke of the heavenly hosts announcing "Glory to God in the highest and on earth peace among men of good will," as the Nirmanakaya body of the Buddha. And so, according to Steiner, the Buddha, who was the first to introduce the principle of peace and compassion to human beings, connects himself intimately with the Nathan Jesus.

When the Nathan Jesus is twelve, the two Jesus children come together in the Temple at Jerusalem, where the two Jesus families are present. At that meeting the Zarathustra ego leaves the body of the Solomon Jesus to become the ego of the Nathan Jesus, which to this point possessed only, as Steiner puts it, a "provisional ego." This accounts, Steiner says, for the radical change in Jesus at the

Temple described in the Gospel of Luke, a change in which the Nathan Jesus, the simple, innocent Adam soul, is suddenly capable of holding his own with the wisdom of the learned men of the Temple, a change at which his parents can only wonder. At that moment in the Temple, Steiner says, the Buddha also enveloped the Nathan Jesus' astral body with his Nirmanakaya body.

Thus, at the time of the baptism in the river Jordan, Jesus embodied the wholeness of the archetypal human being, possessing in his ego all the wisdom acquired on earth by Zarathustra, in his astral body the pure love and compassion of the Buddha, and in his ether body the purity and innocence of the undefiled Adam soul.

IV. The Incarnation and Mystery of Golgotha

At the baptism of Jesus in the Jordan by John, the Zarathustra ego sacrificed itself to the being of the Christ. The Zarathustra ego left the body of the Nathan Jesus and entered the spiritual world, and in its place the Christ being entered the Nathan Jesus as its true ego. This central event is witnessed to by all four gospels. As crucial and central as this moment was, the Incarnation needs to be viewed also as a process, the preparation for which extended back through the centuries and the culmination of which proceeded through the three years of Christ's life on earth, and has continued, and will continue, to develop in its full ramifications throughout the future of earth evolution.

During the three years between the baptism and the crucifixion, the Incarnation of the Christ into the body of Jesus proceeded by stages as the Christ gradually permeated every dimension of Jesus' existence. The permeation of the astral body began immediately after the baptism with the temptations in the wilderness, and is further reflected in the feeding of the 5000 and in Christ's walking on the stormy waves of the lake. As Emil Bock puts it: "It is the astral body completely filled with the Christ ego which now has such intensity that it can reveal itself to the disciples as if it were a constituent part of the sense world." The further permeation by Christ of Jesus' etheric body culminated in the event of the Transfiguration. And, finally, the Christ pressed fully through the physical body, permeating that body, on the one hand, with all the spiritual reality of the Christ but, on the other hand, becoming more and more powerless and given over to the forces of death. This final permeation of the physical realm culminated in the crucifixion and the conquest of death in the resurrection. As the Risen One the Christ is now present as the being of love, joy, peace, and creative transformation in every human individual. He offers himself in freedom to every individual as the ground of the human I, the power for self-transformation, the foundation in love for human community, and the hope and source for the "re-enlivening of the dying earth existence."

V. The Christ Impulse

The Christ does not force himself on anyone. Our personal relationship to the Christ being can only be one of total freedom, for the Christ is the being that grounds the I in total freedom. However, the Christ does work in the world in an objective way, supporting human beings in all their efforts to work for the benefit and future evolution of humanity and of the earth. This objective working of the Christ in the world Rudolf Steiner has described in terms of the working on the earth of "the Christ Impulse."

The Christ is the Logos, the power and being of "creative transformation in love" in the Godhead. In most general terms the Christ Impulse is the working of the Logos as the being of "creative transformation in love and freedom" in earth evolution. Every new creative transformation that breaks through the old and fixed, that opens new possibilities for insight, empathy, and action in love and freedom, can be seen as the working of the Christ.

The concept of the "Christ Impulse" is large, and here it is possible only to suggest in a summary way some primary approaches to understanding it.

1. *The Evolution of Consciousness.* The Christ is the grounding of the I of the human being, carrying the I in its integrity through death and rebirth. As the ground of the I, the Christ undergirds the value, equality, and infinite worth of every individual. The Christ Impulse can be seen at work wherever the evolution of consciousness results in a heightened sense among human beings of their individuality and its potential. Because the freedom of the individual is at stake, the evolution of consciousness is also vulnerable to adversarial powers that would turn individuality to egotism and materialism. Working with the Christ Impulse in the evolution of consciousness means overcoming egoism and recognizing the Christ in the other. The full development of the free individual is the Christ foundation of Waldorf education.

2. *Human Solidarity.* This follows from the above. All the forces working for the recognition of human universality and the overcoming of divisions based on race, nationality, and ideology are expressions of the Christ Impulse. To join with all who are endeavoring to establish human equality and solidarity is to ally oneself with the Christ Impulse.

3. *Regard for the Earth.* In the Mystery of Golgotha the Christ joined with the earth, and all the formative forces of the mineral, plant, and animal worlds were gathered up and transformed in the resurrection body. The manifestation among more and more persons of love and care for the earth, and for the creatures of the earth (for the animals, especially, who in our industrialized cruelty

to them by the millions are desperately in need of mercy and relief), is a working of the Christ Impulse. Waldorf education contains, if Waldorf educators recognize it, a powerful, ecologically based curriculum ideally equipped to foster care of the earth in our time and the actualization of this aspect of the Christ Impulse.

4. *The Transformation of Knowing.* We live in a time in which a mechanistic and materialistic, sense-bound way of knowing is strong, even dominant, in spite of criticisms that have repeatedly been made against it. A narrow, mechanistic, sense-bound way of knowing by definition cannot deal, on the one hand, with values, meaning, and purpose and, on the other hand, with qualities, life, and beauty in nature. A fundamental transformation of knowing is essential if we are ever to face adequately our earth crisis and deal creatively with human conflict. A transformation of knowing that can know qualities in the world with the same rigor that we now know quantities requires a qualitative transformation of ourselves, a transformation that involves the unity and fullness of thinking, feeling, willing, and moral insight. The Christ Impulse is present wherever persons are working for this qualitative transformation of knowing. And this transformation is central to the work of Waldorf education in which a main aim is to help students develop, as an integral whole, all the ways in which we can come to know the world: the participative, the aesthetic, and the conceptual.

5. *Freedom in Love.* The Christ Impulse is present wherever persons are working to establish the reality of freedom in love. This freedom expresses itself both as freedom *from* and freedom *for.* Freedom *from* every form of determinism, whether it derives from the past, from

nature, or from other persons; and freedom *for* the care of and respect for oneself, the other, the earth, and the spirit. "Education for Freedom" is another hallmark of the Christ Impulse in Waldorf education.

Rudolf Steiner said in 1916, at the time of World War I, that "Christianity lives wherever people are able to understand [the] union of all humanity in Christ. In the future, it will not matter much whether what Christ is will still be called by that name. However, a lot will depend on our finding in Christ the spiritual uniter of humanity and accepting that external diversity will increase more and more." Yet, he himself always continued to use the name Christ. Is that, perhaps, because, until a better name is found, this name, despite all of the ways it has been abused and has been used to abuse others, still carries a reminder that the only spirituality appropriate for the truly human is one that involves a real crucifixion and a real resurrection?

Notes

[1] Many readers, for example, will recognize immediately how greatly indebted I am in the second section of these observations, entitled "Historical Background of the Incarnation and Mystery of Golgotha," to the groundbreaking work of Andrew Welburn, especially his book, *The Beginnings of Christianity*, in which he brings together the spiritual research of Rudolf Steiner with modern, mainstream New Testament scholarship, research dealing with the twentieth-century discoveries of the Qum Ran Dead Sea Scrolls in Israel, and the Nag Hammadi manuscripts in Egypt. Most of this section is drawn directly from Welburn, but I am, of course, responsible for any misunderstandings of his work that I may have committed.

[2] The main sources for this section are the two lectures by Rudolf Steiner, *Pre-Earthly Deeds of Christ* and *The Four Sacrifices of Christ*.

References

Barfield, Owen. *Saving the Appearances: A Study in Idolatry.* New York: Harcourt Brace Jovanovich, n.d.

Bock, Emil. *The Three Years: The Life of Christ Between Baptism and Ascension.* Edinburgh: Floris Books, 1987.

Steiner, Rudolf. *Christianity as Mystical Fact and the Mysteries of Antiquity.* Hudson, NY: Anthroposophic Press, 1972.

_____. *The Fifth Gospel.* London: Rudolf Steiner Publishing, 1950.

_____. *Pre-Earthly Deeds of Christ.* North Vancouver: Steiner Book Centre, 1947.

_____. *The Four Sacrifices of Christ.* Spring Valley, NY: Anthroposophic Press, 1944.

Welburn, Andrew. *The Beginnings of Christianity: Essene Mystery, Gnostic Revelation and the Christian Vision.* Edinburgh: Floris Books, 1991.

How Do Teachers Transform Themselves and Come to Experience the Christ Impulse?

Betty Staley

One of the key responsibilities of being a Waldorf teacher is the willingness to work on one's own self-transformation. What does this entail? After all, no one can coerce a teacher to tread the path of self-improvement. No one will keep track of how often a teacher does the nightly meditation. The desire for self-transformation must arise from out of the teacher's inner longing to develop his or her higher self.

There are three main reasons for the teacher to work on self-transformation:
· strengthening one's perceptive capacities to see the true nature of the child
· warming one's connection with the child's angel
· becoming a more effective supporter of the child's growth through the curriculum and one's teaching

The teacher's renewal directly affects the child's own transformation through its stages of growth and development. Beyond the individual child, the teacher's growing sensitivity also helps the class develop into a healthy organism. And through the teachers' working together — awakening and practicing their social skills, strengthening their connection to the spirit of the school — the faculty becomes a healthy vessel in which the spirit of the school can become manifest.

Only during the very last years of his life did Rudolf Steiner mention explicitly the importance of the Christ Impulse in Waldorf pedagogy. For instance, in the lecture cycle entitled *The Child's Changing Consciousness* (Lecture 6), he characterizes the selfless attitude that the teacher should cultivate in relation to the child: "Dear God, make that I, as far as my personal ambitions are concerned, quite obliterate myself. And Christ make true in me the Pauline word, 'Not I, but the Christ in me' . . . . that the Holy Spirit may hold sway in the teacher."[1] But in his published books, such as Theosophy, How to Know Higher Worlds, and Intuitive Thinking as a Spiritual Path: A Philosophy of Freedom, as well as in the Teacher's Imagination and in the two Teacher's Meditations, Rudolf Steiner makes no mention of the Christ by name. Isn't this surprising? And yet, the most profound spiritual truths are presented in these books, lectures, and meditations. This omission may serve as a clue to our exploration.

Indeed, Rudolf Steiner was clear that the name Christ can be overused. In Lecture 8 of the cycle quoted above, he says: "There is no need to have the name of the Lord constantly upon one's lips nor of calling upon the name of Christ all the time. . . . Nevertheless, it is possible to permeate one's entire life with a fundamental religious impulse, with a most intensely Christian impulse. Then certain experiences of old, no longer known to modern intellectuality, will begin to stir in one's soul."[2]

In sweeping away references to Christ, at least as they are used by religious denominations, perhaps Rudolf Steiner is preparing the ground for a new understanding of the Christ, a ground more appropriate for the period of the Consciousness Soul in which we live. Perhaps he is showing us that we can relate to the deepest questions of spiritual existence without relying on the name "Christ", which has been abused both by sacred traditions and by a long string of secular customs, such as the barrage of Christmas carols that can be heard blaring from shopping mall loudspeakers each year. Rudolf Steiner is pointing to something new in human understanding that has nothing to do with dogma, with rules, or with religious coercion, but rather with freedom as each of us comes to our own understanding of and relationship to spiritual knowledge and the Christ.

When we refer to the Christ, we can take three different aspects into consideration – the Christ Event, Esoteric Christianity, and the Christ Impulse – and none of these refers specifically to organized Christianity.

*   *First, there is the Christ Event in human history.* This arises out of the ancient mysteries. Here Rudolf Steiner describes the Christ as a spiritual being who gradually draws closer to the earth, inspiring the great initiates in different cultures, until finally He incarnates into the body of the person Jesus. This event Rudolf Steiner describes as "the turning point of time". Human culture, he says, had become increasingly materialistic to the point that it had lost sight of its connection to the spiritual world. The dangers to humanity's life on earth arising from this situation were so great that the Christ had to incarnate into physical form in order that people could experience their relationship to the higher worlds. Had the Christ not taken on human physical form, human intelligence would have become thoroughly one-sided, and human beings would have lost their way in the darkness of materialism. When we speak, then, of the Christ Event, we are speaking of the Incarnation, the Life, Death, and Resurrection of the Christ.

*   *Second, there is Esoteric Christianity.* Here we are referring to esoteric streams of teaching, including Anthroposophy. The task here is to understand what was living in the mystery centers, to explore the deeper aspects of Christianity which were either pushed out of traditional Christianity or considered heretical by those Christian sects that declared themselves to be the authority on the Christ. Esoteric Christianity has the task of keeping alive an awareness of the Christ Impulse as that which united Itself with the Earth, making it possible for every human being to partake of healing, compassion, and love.

*   *The third aspect is the Christ Impulse.* Rudolf Steiner characterizes the Christ Impulse as a lofty spiritual being, the Holy Spirit, that entered into Jesus at the Baptism in Jordan. In this sense the Christ Impulse is the continued working of the Christ in the hearts and minds of all people, everywhere on the earth. This Impulse works in the heart, creating a balance between the Luciferic and Ahrimanic forces. The statue carved by Rudolf Steiner, called the Representative of Humanity, shows a figure standing between two forces. We can say, on the one hand, that this giant statue is a representation of the Christ, but we can also say that is a representation of every human being.

These three aspects are all significantly different from organized Christianity. The Christ Event is an objective occurrence worthy of study and understanding. Esoteric Christianity is available for those interested in going behind the traditional view of Christianity into deeper spiritual research. The Christ Impulse works all over the world, inspiring transformation, renewal, brotherhood, and love. However, it is difficult in American society (and also in our schools) to be clear about these differences. When we refer to the "Christianizing of society" or say that something was a particularly "Christian impulse", we need to be really clear what we mean and what we do not mean. Often when we speak about divine forces, the working of God, the universal impulse of love and forgiveness, we may be speaking about the Christ Impulse, and yet this name may close off those who think we are speaking out of a sectarian viewpoint.

How, then, can we find a path that leads to the Christ Impulse without becoming sidetracked by sectarian misunderstanding? One of Rudolf Steiner's verses, "Victorious Spirit", says it in this way, though once again without direct reference to the Christ:

Victorious Spirit
Flame through the impotence of irresolute souls.
Burn out the egoism,
Ignite the compassion,
That selflessness, the lifestream of humankind,
Wells up as the source of spirit rebirth.[3]

Overcoming egoism, igniting compassion – these are two vital qualities for the Waldorf teacher. In working with this verse, we are reminded that in self-overcoming, we make ourselves into a vessel, we become spiritually strong.

If we recall the children's morning verses and also the teacher's meditations, we will notice that here, too, Rudolf Steiner does not use the word Christ, and yet they irradiate our lives with the work of the Christ Impulse. For example, every morning the children of the first four grades proclaim

That I with all my might
May love to work and learn.
From thee come light and strength,
To thee rise love and thanks.

From fifth grade through the senior year of high school, the students speak these words at the start of each day:

To Thee, Creator Spirit,
I will now turn my heart
To ask that strength and grace and skill
For learning and for work
In me may live and grow.

In these verses the children and the students reach out to their better selves in a promise of transformation and renewal that Steiner speaks of as the Christ Impulse. In a word, these transformative qualities of the Christ Impulse can be summed up by the term "brotherhood."

In a lecture cycle entitled *Brotherhood and the Struggle for Existence* (1905), Rudolf Steiner speaks of two impulses in the world: brotherhood based on human love that transcends race, sex, profession, and religion; and the struggle for existence arising from one's own sense of survival. How do we strengthen the forces of brotherhood? Through working together in communities, in associations, for the greater good. "The new entity arises only when the one lives in the other, when the single individual draws strength not only from himself, but also from others. Only if each lives selflessly in the other."[4]

Our future task is to establish brotherhoods out of the highest ideals of the soul. But how do we achieve this goal? We can begin by learning to respect the freedom of someone else's thoughts, even when we think that person is incorrect. We have to learn to listen with the soul, not only with the word. We can develop our talents individually, but to develop our character we need to work within a community. It is in the community that we have the meaning of "When two or three are gathered. . . ."

The Christ Impulse is an expression or a gift of the Holy Spirit. It works through time, through transformation and renewal, through love, sacrifice, and forgiveness. It awakens the best in us, it allows us to find what is human in the other person, so that we can meet the spiritual nature, the "truly human" in our fellow human beings. This Impulse is working whenever we are involved in a process of transformation, whenever we help another person find what is truly human, whenever we overcome our own prejudice or help the children overcome theirs.

In another lecture, known as *The Work of the Angels in Man's Astral Body*, Rudolf Steiner predicts that traditional religion will pass away and the meeting of two people will be experienced as a sacrament.[5] This is also a description of the working of the Christ Impulse, even if the word Christ is not even used.

In other lectures, Steiner describes how the process of birth leads to God, and re-birth leads to Christ. He tells the teachers they must make it possible for every child, in the course of his or her life, to find the Christ Impulse, in order to experience an inner re-birth. When we help children grow and transform their capacities, from selfishness to altruism, from pride in their own efforts to a delight in the achievements of others, we are helping to foster a re-birth in the children.

When as a teacher I respect the freedom of someone else's thought, when I learn to listen not just with my mind but with my soul — that is, not only to the words but the feelings behind the words — I am seeking within myself the Christ-Impulse.

So far, we have been speaking in terms of heart, brotherhood, re-birth, seeing the divine in the other, transformation, respect beyond race, religion, profession. These words sound very modern. When we think now about the world today and try to identify moral leaders who embody these words, we can think of Mahatma Gandhi, of Martin Luther King, Jr., of Andrei Sakharov, of Mother Theresa, of Nelson Mandela, of Rachel Carson, of Jane Goodall, and many others. What they share is their transformation of certain experiences. Out of their transformed experiences a new understanding was born that spoke to human beings all over the world. They embody the moral conscience of our time.

How are we to grasp this new understanding? The Christ Impulse is expressed whenever teachers nurture the best in themselves, when they awaken love, sacrifice, and forgiveness in their relationship with children, with parents, and with colleagues.

How do we do this? Rudolf Steiner has given us many different exercises to help us develop a new sacrament in our work. These include developing objectivity about oneself, seeing the divine in the other, and listening deeply to the other. First let us concentrate on our work with the children.

The first exercise in this work is the Review of the Day. In this exercise we create images of the main events of the day, starting from the evening and moving step by step towards the morning. Through this exercise, we see ourselves from outside, which allows us to become separate from the emotions that we felt at the moment of contact. We can begin to see patterns emerging in our behavior with certain children, and we can come to recognize our initial reaction that leads to these patterns. This exercise, practiced regularly, awakens self-consciousness and helps us to respond more sensitively and appropriately.

A second exercise involves the practice of open-mindedness so that we can overcome prejudices and open ourselves to the true I of the child. We ask ourselves, "Can I see the divine in the child? Or am I embedded in my own subconscious biases?" We explore the prejudices having to do with race, religion, gender, or particular habits that may lurk in the shadows of our soul. We confront ourselves with the question, "Do certain children irritate me while other children are my favorites?"

A third exercise for working with children is to practice deep soul listening. We ask, "What does this child need from me?" By working with the child's angel, we can begin to hear what the child needs. Although this form of listening is very subtle, it is also very powerful.

Now, let us turn to our relationship with colleagues. The same qualities we develop for working with the children can help us in our relationship with fellow teachers. The Review of the Day exercise can help us recognize our typical reaction when a particular colleague speaks in the faculty meeting, or when we are working on a committee to design a school festival. Gaining objectivity in my relationships with colleagues is a helpful starting point.

How do I open myself to the divine in the colleague? I become interested in my colleague. I discover some of his or her gifts, I find something to admire about his or her work in the class or school. I ask myself, "Which prejudices do I hold of my colleagues? Are there certain colleagues whose ideas I ignore repeatedly, prejudging that nothing of real value will emerge? Or are there other colleagues with whom I feel so much sympathy that I always agree with their ideas? Did I develop an attitude toward the colleague based on first impressions, or was it something that happened more recently? Can I get beyond the old impression so as to see my colleague in a fresh and new way?"

How can I develop deep soul listening? I ask myself, "Am I really hearing the intention beyond the words as well as the words themselves?" Or I can say to myself, "What is my colleague needing? How can I enhance his or her work?"

To be sure, many of us have had the experience of listening to one another in a deep way. This can happen when one teacher gives away his or her own ideas and becomes one with those of another. These moments, these sacred moments are expressions of the Christ Impulse working within a group.

One such experience stands out for me. In our College of Teachers we were trying to choose a new first grade teacher. Two candidates were being considered, but we could not decide which one was right. During the first week most of the group supported one candidate; the next week the support swayed to the other. After more than a month of trying to come to a conclusion, we realized that neither candidate was right for this class. Once we had come to this clarity as a group – and this realization came in an instant – we were open to considering a third candidate who had not even applied. We met this third person, and within minutes it was obvious that here was the right teacher. In retrospect we realized that in setting aside our initial likes and dislikes and listening instead to something higher than ourselves, at one special moment something beyond each of us had entered the room.

Another aspect of experiencing the divine in the colleagues can occur when we give up our own viewpoint and think of the greater good of the school. Out of this, love can flow. One particular example illustrates this. A teacher had been working effectively in the school for many years. One day she lost her temper and hit a child. You can just imagine the phone calls and meetings that flowed from this situation – with parents, with colleagues, and perhaps with the child. Over the years we had experienced other situations in which we had had to confront teachers because of their behavior. If a teacher was asked to leave the school, often this dismissal happened under a dark cloud. Guilt, anger, frustration, shame, and disappointment overshadowed these difficult decisions, and in the aftermath colleagues experienced coldness and aloofness in their relationships. In this case, however, the teacher came to the College of Teachers the same day and said that she was in the wrong, that she had been losing her temper more often, and that for the good of the children and the school, it was time for her to step down. A feeling of gratitude from the colleagues poured forth. The teacher's self-understanding, her willingness to take responsibility for her actions and not subject the school to greater difficulties created warmth and love. Rather than feeling unwelcome on the school campus, as had happened in other situations, this teacher was invited subsequently to many functions and was always embraced with love.

The "Teacher's Imagination", given by Rudolf Steiner to the faculty of the original Waldorf school, provides one of the strongest pictures of how to develop a sacred relationship with colleagues. In particular the reference to the archangels weaving from one human being to the other, passing on what each has to give to the other, can inspire gratitude and appreciation for our colleagues.

Another aspect of the Christ Impulse is active when we recognize the freedom of another person's thoughts. We may disagree with a colleague, but we nevertheless respect the fact that he or she has freedom of thinking. We cannot impose our thoughts on another person. We cannot try to make a colleague become a clone of ourselves. We can offer different viewpoints, we can try to convince; but in the final analysis we need to respect the other person's thoughts as being his or her own.

Having looked at practices involving the children and the colleagues, let us look now to our working with parents. Let's imagine that a parent calls with a concern. Perhaps our first response is to become defensive, or even to go on the attack. "What did I do wrong?" we say, or "Why are you so critical?" As we know well, perhaps from painful experience, neither response is helpful. Instead, if we can agree at the outset that we share similar concerns for the healthy development of the child, we may be able to reach an understanding of what happened and what needs to happen with the concern brought by the parent. In this case, I ask myself, "Can I listen and hear what is behind the words? Or am I going to quibble about particular words that the parent used to express this concern? Can I recognize the divine in the parent even if I don't agree with his or her viewpoint?" If we can transform the mood of the exchange from antagonism to partnership, we can work together for the good of the child. Particularly helpful in cases like these are the practices of positivity, open-mindedness, and compassion that Rudolf Steiner offered as part of a series of six so-called "basic exercises" for inner development.

In our work with parents it is important to keep a quality of "I-Thou" rather than "I-It" in our relationships. Parents are individuals. Each is looking out for the best interests of her or his child. That is the parent's job. Our task is to listen and suggest ways of working together so that we can do our job more effectively. We need to free ourselves from the past or from feeling,

"Here we go again with another round of complaints." For this feeling locks us into past perceptions and robs us of an ability to perceive the situation in its new reality. Deep soul listening is needed in order to stay in the moment.

In our dealings as teachers with the children, with our colleagues (fellow teachers and staff members), and with the parents, we are working out of our higher self and its transformation of the lower self. This process, working through time, gives birth to new faculties. These are signs of the working of the Christ Impulse – renewal, love, sacrifice, forgiveness, and compassion.

In order to seek the divine in the other person, we have to find a relationship to the divine in ourselves. This can happen through the connection we forge in our meditative life, in our experiences of nature, in the study of spiritual matters, and in service to others. The evening Teacher's Meditation powerfully connects us with our higher self, as does the verse "Victorious Spirit" cited earlier.

The Christ Impulse lives and works on many levels – in historical unfolding, in everyday life, in our relationships to one another, to oneself, and to nature. The Christ Impulse is not separate from us. In fact, our every deed affects the Christ Impulse in a profound way.

What we create through deeds of faith and trust, deeds performed out of wonder and astonishment, is given over to the Christ-Ego (the Christ Impulse) and forms a spiritual sheath that we can compare to our astral body.

When our deeds are transformed into deeds of love, we help to build the etheric body of the Christ Impulse.

And whatever we create in the world based on conscience builds for the Christ Impulse that which corresponds to the human physical body.

Thus the Christ Impulse is in us and we are in the Christ Impulse.

The verses, meditations, and exercises described above help us to remember our true calling as teacher – namely to discover what is human in the child, to recognize the gifts of the child, to see the divine in the child. In this way we serve the child in his or her development. It is a noble calling. In order to develop these capacities, we must work through the development of our heart forces and our trust in the spiritual world. This is the new sacrament, the working of the Christ Impulse in our tasks as teachers.

References

1. Rudolf Steiner, *The Child's Changing Consciousness and Waldorf Education* (Hudson, NY: Anthroposophic Press, 1988), lecture 6, p. 146.
2. Ibid., lecture 8, pp. 182-183.
3. Rudolf Steiner, "Victorious Spirit," for another translation of this verse, see *Guidance in Esoteric Training* (London: Rudolf Steiner Press, 1972), p.70.
4. Rudolf Steiner, *Brotherhood and the Struggle for Existence* (Spring Valley, NY: Mercury Press, n.d.), p. 9.
5. Rudolf Steiner, *The Work of the Angels in Man's Astral Body* (London: Rudolf Steiner Press, 1960), p. 16.

The Chariot of Michael

Dorit Winter

Is Michaelmas a Christian Festival? Yes and no.

"During the Middle Ages, Michaelmas was a great religious feast and many popular traditions grew up around the day, which coincided with the harvest in much of Western Europe."[1] It is still a Feast Day in the church, but there is hardly any awareness of the day's significance, or even of its existence, in our culture at large. By comparison to Easter or Christmas, it is invisible.

Is Michaelmas connected to what Rudolf Steiner calls the Christ Impulse? Most emphatically yes.

It is this disparity which causes so much hesitancy in our schools. We celebrate the day with gusto. Typically, the entire school is involved. If we are in a rural school, we delight in the outdoor drama, sometimes complete with a real horse and rider. In many of our schools, there is a play, or playlet, often carried by the Second Grade, often complete with animated dragon which necessitates a somewhat simplified version of what we are celebrating. The second grade curriculum includes saints. The children's Michaelmas production revolves around St. George. Sometimes there is genuine confusion, and there is reference to Saint Michaël. But Michaël is not a saint. Saints are human beings, albeit special human beings, who through their own strivings, have purified their lower nature. In anthroposophical circles, the name of Michaël is pronounced with the emphasis on the last syllable, to remind us that he is not just Michael, but a spiritual being, an Archangel. He shares the last syllable of his name with other heavenly beings: Raphaël, Gabriël, Uriël, and even Elohim. Rudolf

Steiner, in many different lectures, explains that there are seven
Archangels who take turns as "Regent of the Time," or Archai.
Michaël's "reign" began in 1879 and will last until 2239. He is
now the spiritual being attending the cosmic development of
humanity. It is no coincidence that anthroposophy emerged in his
reign.

For Rudolf Steiner, the connection between Michaelmas,
Michaël, and the Christ Impulse was straightforward. On the day
before Michaelmas, 1924, Rudolf Steiner culminated a lifetime of
lecturing activity with a mighty proclamation: "The Michaël Power
and the Michaël Will are none other than the Christ Will and the
Christ Power." He went on to speak of the "Michaël mood," the
"Michaël Thought," the "Michaël garment," a garment of light.
"This Michaël garment, this garment of Light, shall become the
Words of the Worlds, which are the Christ Words – the Words of
the Worlds, which can transform the Logos of the Worlds into the
Logos of Humankind."[2] Then follows the mantram known as the
"Michaël Imagination." In it Michaël is called the "messenger of
Christ," the "herald of Christ." The Michaël Verse is Rudolf Steiner's
last Logos to us. Its message of Light, Life, and Love[3] can be
received as a seed to germinate and infuse every aspect of
anthroposophical work – including the pedagogical work.

When we celebrate Michaelmas, we are celebrating the Christ
Impulse. As teachers we should not have any doubts as to what
we are doing. We are not celebrating the story of St. George and
the Dragon. George (who was claimed by the church as a saint,
and thus deprived of his cosmic heritage), and the story of the
dragon he slays to save a village, are earthly cloaks for mighty,
cosmic, spiritual realities.

But then, our entire Waldorf curriculum is an earthly picture
of mighty, cosmic, spiritual realities. Or should be.

There are several levels: At the highest level, there is the Logos, which streams toward humanity from the sun. "In its purest form, this external physical body of the Logos appears especially in the outer sunlight. But the sunlight is not merely material light. To spiritual perception, it is just as much the vesture of the Logos, as your outer physical body is the vesture of your soul." In short: "Everything is an incarnation of the Logos."[4]

At the next level, this Logos/Light incarnated into human flesh: "The inner force of the sun, the force of the Logos-Love assumed a physical human form in the body of Jesus of Nazareth. For, like an external object, like an outer being, God had to appear to the earthly, human sense-consciousness in a bodily form."[5]

Then comes the level which leads us closer to home: "Anthroposophy is, in all details, a striving to imbuing-with-the-Christ-impulse [*Durchchristung*] the world."[6]

Now we have traveled from the source to the prime incarnation, and thence to its manifestation, which becomes our source.

And that brings us to the level which is our province: Waldorf education. For, like anthroposophy itself, the Waldorf curriculum – meaning not just the subjects, but everything we do with the children – becomes ever richer the more our research and consciousness embrace its source. And its source is, on the one hand, the growing child and, on the other, the universe – both as recognized by spiritual science.

There is a continuum and an integration of these various levels which must become apparent to one who penetrates the work of Rudolf Steiner, yet so sensitive are our schools to the sting of the epithet "religious" that, in our attempt to avoid it, we become removed from our source, anthroposophy, let alone its source, the Christ Impulse. It is not far-fetched to say that anthroposophy is the Logos of the consciousness soul, and its garment is Waldorf education. Here is Rudolf Steiner's picture for this: "Michaël *needs*, as it were, a chariot by means of which to enter our civilization. . . . By educating in the right way we are preparing Michaël's chariot for his entrance into our civilization"[7] [emphasis added]. In other words, as the entire lecture cycle (*The Younger Generation,* from which these words are taken) makes clear, Waldorf education is the vehicle for Michaël, the "Messenger of Christ," the "Herald of Christ." But that is so only when Waldorf education allows the Logos-Light of anthroposophy to shine through its curriculum. That is why Waldorf can never become a method. The more conscious the Waldorf teacher is of the Light which illuminates our curriculum, the more the Waldorf teacher successfully "fuels" Michaël's chariot, the more the Waldorf teacher raises the child.

But how is this to be achieved?

It can become a source of joy and satisfaction to find, in the vast body of Rudolf Steiner's lectures apart from the pedagogical lectures, references to the curriculum. Such references are not meant as indications for the Waldorf curriculum, but nevertheless, that is what they are.

Following are examples for each step in our curriculum. The references quoted have been gathered over the past seven years or so since I started keeping a binder with one index for grade levels, another for curriculum topics. Although there is a website (for now in German only) where any word in the entire bibliography of Rudolf Steiner's work can be looked up and all references provided, slow and steady research through one's own reading of entire lecture cycles or books will, ultimately, yield greater benefits. The planned publication of this entire bibliography in English will make such personal research all the more accessible.

Appropriately enough, our example for **Grade One** is related to the "AlphaBet". How much richer the teaching of the letters can be when the teacher contemplates the following:

> *In writings such as John's Book of Revelation many things are still expressed in the language of the mysteries, so they can only be understood if the meaning can be extricated out of the Mystery language. It is not surprising that the writer of the Book of Revelation spoke in the Mystery language, for in his day people were still familiar with it. They knew that the sounds of speech are supersensible beings,* **that Alpha is the human being as a supersensible being at the beginning of his existence, that when you move from Alpha to Beta you move from human being to world, including the divine world, and that when you go through all the sounds of the alphabet to Omega you are taking into yourself the whole of the divine world** *[emphasis added] . . . . You do not know very much if you only know the ABC. Such things are trifles, but they are trifles that point back to a beginning where there were divine, spiritual beings. Our trifling letters of the alphabet are the descendents of what humanity once upon a time recognized as divine, spiritual beings.*[8]

A short excerpt does not do this reference justice. It comes in the context of a review of planetary evolution, in a lecture cycle given to priests. One page before this excerpt, Rudolf Steiner asks: "When the human being was still a being of warmth [on Old Saturn], what did his inner experiences look like subjectively in the soul?" His answer: "His inner experience was pure wonderment about the world." And then the two conditions are united: "Warmth cannot be comprehended as anything other than pure wonderment." And then several sentence further: "This is the Alpha: the Saturn human being, the warmth human being living in wonderment." There we have it, although it takes two more pages to crystallize: "*Alpha is the human being as a supersensible being at the beginning of his existence.*" And, immediately following this characterization of "the warmth human being living in wonderment," comes Beta: "And the first thing the human being experienced as world, as the outer housing provided by the world, the skin, this is Beta, the human being in his house, in his temple." Then follows a paragraph about the evolution of man from Saturn through until Vulcan, from Alpha to Omega. "At the end of the Vulcan condition, the human being too will be permitted to say: I am Alpha and Omega."

And now Rudolf Steiner says, "Let us look at what we have imagined to ourselves as being the beginning, middle and end of humanity's evolution, let us look at this in conjunction with the Mystery of Golgotha. In the being who incarnated in Jesus through the Mystery of Golgotha we have – roughly half way thorough human evolution – a being in the world who is already at the stage in world evolution that the human being will have reached at the end of the Vulcan condition. We have a being as a god such as man will be as a human being at the end of the Vulcan condition."

And then, two paragraphs later, comes the excerpt cited above concerning the ABC.

Three lectures on, Rudolf Steiner returns to the alphabet, this time to distinguish the vowels from the consonants in this way: "Of these 32 sounds it is easy to work out that about 24 are consonants and about seven are vowels – of course such things are always approximate. . . . you can then throw light on the image . . . of the Alpha and the Omega surrounded by the seven angels – the vowels – and the 24 elders – the consonants."[9] Angels and Elders! These are presences from the Book of Revelation, and it goes without saying that such images are for the teacher to contemplate, and not for the children to receive directly. But what a picture it is for the teacher. What an example of how to find the picture, which every first grade teacher is always seeking, when presenting these Angels and Elders.

On the very same page, Rudolf Steiner then turns to numbers: "It is the same with numbers. Our present idea of numbers is thoroughly abstract. . . . [In] the Book of Revelation . . . there was still a feeling for the secret of numbers. . . . People experienced what was contained in the three, in the four; they experienced the closed nature of the three, the open nature of the four, the nature of the five, so closely related to the being of man. Something divine was felt to be in numbers, just as something divine was also found in the written letters and in the sounds of speech."

There are five major lecture cycles which deal directly with the John Gospel or The Apocalypse by John. A first grade teacher can find in them endlessly fertile substrata for an understanding of "our trifling letters of the alphabet." With such riches underfoot, the teacher's entire stance in the classroom cannot but partake of that primal warmth and wonderment which, ultimately, is what educates the child. And, as even a little bit of digging will reveal, this warmth and wonderment, when it is informed by consciousness of its source, *is* the Christ Impulse.

For consideration of our theme in the second grade, we can look at one of the saints: Saint Francis. Rudolf Steiner devoted a lecture cycle to him: *Francis of Assisi and the Mission of Love.* That is the subtitle. Both the earthly and the spiritual biographies of Francis are presented. We hear about the life of Francis, his birth, his youth, his transformation from knight to healer. "The young knight who in his boldest dreams had only longed to become a great warrior was transformed into a man who now most earnestly sought all the impulses of mercy, compassion and love. All the forces he had thought of using in the physical world were transformed into moral impulses of the inner world." In the second lecture we learn how this transformation is related to the spiritual convergence of the Buddha's teaching with the individuality of Francis.

On the shores of the Black Sea there existed an occult school which lasted far into the Christian era. This school was guided by certain human beings who set themselves as their highest ideal that part of the teaching of Buddha which we have just described, and through their having taken into themselves the Christian impulse along with it, were able in the early centuries of Christianity to throw new light upon what Buddha had given to humanity. . . . From this school proceeded two groups, as it were, one group which possessed the impulse to carry the teaching of Buddha everywhere, although his name was not mentioned in connection with it, and a second group which, in addition, received the Christ-impulse. Now the difference between these two kinds did not appear very strongly in that particular incarnation, it only appeared in the next. The pupils who had not received the Christ-impulse but who had only gained the Buddha-impulse, became the teachers of the equality and brotherhood of man; on the other hand the pupils who had also received the Christ-impulse, in the next incarnation were such that this Christ-impulse worked on further so that not only could they teach (and they did not consider this their chief task) but they worked more especially through their moral power. One such pupil of the occult school on the Black Sea was born in his next incarnation as Francis of Assisi. No wonder, then, that in him there was the wisdom which he had received, the knowledge of the brotherhood of mankind, of the equality of all men, of the necessity to love all men equally, no wonder that this teaching pulsated through his soul and also that his soul was permeated and strengthened by the Christ-impulse.[10]

Rudolf Steiner then goes on to explain how it was that Francis was able to heal. "Now how did this Christ-impulse work further in his next incarnation? It acted in such a way that, when in his next incarnation Francis of Assisi was transposed into a community in which the old demons of diseases were especially active — this Christ-impulse approached the evil substance of the disease-demons through him, and absorbed it into itself, thus removing it from mankind...." Even more specifically, "his moral forces thereby became so strong that they could take away the harmful spiritual substances which had produced the disease." Then there is further elucidation of how the Christ Impulse enters the life of Francis:

"Consider the life of Francis of Assisi. . . . From his fourteenth year, at the dawn of his astral life the Christ power became particularly active within him, in such a way that there entered into his astral body that which had been in connection with the atmosphere of the earth since the Mystery of Golgotha. For Francis of Assisi was a personality who was permeated by the external power of Christ, owing to his having sought for the Christ power, in his previous incarnation, in that particular place of initiation where it was to be found."

The third lecture shows us how *foolhardiness* and *cowardice*, two possible mis-directions of freedom of the will that lived in the ancient Mysteries, became, in Francis of Assisi, *bravery* and *valor*. These were, in turn, transformed into *love* guided by *wisdom*. At the center of this transformation, which stretches across the evolution of humanity in the post-atlantean epochs, lies the Christ Impulse. It is a beautiful lecture. The entire lecture cycle will profoundly alter the second grade teacher's grasp of the topic. Before leaving this theme, one more short and provocative quotation:

> *St. Francis of Assisi and Thomas Aquinas had woven into their beings copies of the astral body of Jesus of Nazareth. It is this fact that enabled them to exercise such powerful influences as teachers. They worked out of a sphere in which Christ had once lived.*[11]

The child experiencing the "nine year change" requires a further incarnation of the impulse we have been tracking. "Old Testament" is one of the **third grade** curriculum indications – at least in our hemisphere and on our continent. Why? Often we hear that the child at this age needs an example of a great authority, and can feel this reflected in the God of the Old Testament, Jahve. But there is much more to it. Here is one reference, from the dozens that could be cited:

*The relations of all other peoples to their gods were different from
those of the Jews to their Jahve. The other relations were predetermined:
they reflected the outcome of the relations of men to the spirits of the
higher Hierarchies during the Saturn, Sun and Moon period. The Jewish
people had the task of developing a relationship that belonged specially to
the Earth period, but when the Ego wishes to establish a relationship
with its god, how does this find expression? Not as inspiration, so that
morality springs from the operation of divine forces within the soul, but as
commandment. . . . The commandments that arise when the Ego
stands directly over against God and receives from God the rule, the
precept, that the Ego must follow out of its own inner will – this kind of
commandment is met with first among the Jewish people. And it is here,
too, that we first find God entering into a covenant with his people.*[12]

Covenant is the key word. Second graders are not yet ready
for such an arrangement; third graders can find something worthy
to attend to when their teachers' expectations include such an
implicit (not explicit) understanding.

Rudolf Steiner elucidates the concept of Jahve in many different
lecture cycles. It is well nigh impossible to explain the concept out
of context – not for nothing did Rudolf Steiner devote so many
lectures to this theme; it is tightly woven into the entire evolution
of humanity.

*When the ancient Moon had completed its evolution, there were
seven great beings . . . who had progressed far enough to pour forth love.
. . . Seven principle Spirits of Light, who at the same time were the
dispensing Spirits of Love, were able to evolve upon this sun. Only six of
them, however, made the sun their dwelling-place and what streams down
to us in the physical light of the sun contains within it the spiritual force
of love from these six Spirits of Light, or as they are called in the Bible, the
six Elohim. One separated from the others and took a different path for
the salvation of humanity. He did not choose the sun but the moon for his
abode. And this Spirit of Light, who voluntarily renounced life upon the
sun and chose the moon instead, is none other than the one whom the Old
Testament calls "Jahve" or "Jehovah." This Spirit of Light who chose
the moon as a dwelling-place is the one who from there pours ripened
wisdom down upon the earth, thus preparing the way for love.*[13]

And then, two pages later, we learn that what Jahve was preparing was "an actual incarnation of the six sun Elohim, [of] the Logos."

This is, as the whole of the lecture cycles on the John Gospel makes clear, the cosmic relationship of Old to New Testament. Any and all of the Old Testament stories have endlessly profound underpinnings, whether we are talking about Abraham, about Cain and Abel, about Moses or any other. And in a related lecture cycle about the Book of Revelation by John, there is a marvelous cross reference, linking two parts of the third grade curriculum, and thus explaining, at the deepest level, their connection to each other and to the child at this stage of development:

> *The concept of building dwellings merged with the concept of building one's body. This was a beautiful, a wonderfully beautiful picture, for it is also quite practical. The body in which deeds were done and where soul processes and functions took place was a house, and the external house provided protection for all of this. There was this wonderful picture: If I build a house from earthly materials for my external activities, then the walls of the house, the house as a whole, provides a protection for what I do. This is merely an expanded, or you could say a hardened, a more sclerotic continuation of the first house the human being built — the first house, the one that contained the inner processes of soul, is his body. Having built his body, which is a house, he then builds a second house, which uses ingredients from the earth as building materials. It was considered a perfectly everyday matter to regard the body as a house, and this house as the protective garment donned by the human being here in the physical, earthly world. What is formed out of the soul like this was regarded as the house building done by the human being.*[14]

For our consideration of **Grade Four**, we have marvelous choices. There are, to mention two main lessons, cosmic references to the Man and Animal block, and to the Norse Myths:

In his lecture cycle entitled *The Gospel of St. John In Its Relation to the Other Three Gospels*, Rudolf Steiner traces the pre-history of the four spiritual streams which eventually evolve into the four gospels, into the four symbols for these gospels, into the four species that symbolize them: the eagle, the lion, the cow, and the human being.

> *The bull, the lion, the eagle and the human being as related to the ancient mysteries and connected to the Gospels of Luke, Mark, John and Matthew, respectively.*[15]

Or:

> *There are four chief universal powers, to which Christianity gives a new direction: War (the lion); Peaceful Work (the bull); Justice (the being with the human face); and Religious Ardor (the eagle).*[16]

Either one of these would give the fourth grade teacher an entirely unexpected scope when characterizing the animals. True, in the seventh lecture of *Practical Advice to Teachers*, Rudolf Steiner provides concrete and specific explanations for this curriculum block. He also explains why this topic constitutes the first lessons on natural history and why it comes now, in fourth grade, and not earlier. But the quotation that follows gives a broader context, a cosmic context:

> *It is the same in evolution. The lowest animals were unable to wait, they left their spiritual mother-substance too early and hence have thus remained behind at an earlier stage of evolution. Thus the gradually ascending grades of lower beings represent backward stages in evolution. Man waited until the last; he was the last to leave his spiritual, divine mother-substance and descend as a dense substance in fleshly form. The animals descended earlier and therefore remained at that stage. . . . The animal forms have remained at a standstill; they have left the spiritual germ; they have separated themselves and are now degenerating. They represent a branch of the great tree of humanity. In ancient times man*

had the various animal natures within him, as it were, but then separated them off one after another as side branches. All the animals in their different forms represent nothing other than human passions which condensed too early. What man still possesses spiritually in his astral body, the several animal forms represent physically. He kept this in his astral body until the latest period of earth existence, and hence he could progress the furthest.

And now we move into the future, and we find that a further extrusion will take place:

Man still has something within him which must separate itself from sensual evolution as a descending branch, as the other animal forms have done. What man has within him as tendencies to good and evil, to cleverness and stupidity, to beauty and ugliness, represents the possibility of an upward progress or a remaining behind. Just as the animal form has developed out of progressing mankind, so will the race of evil . . . develop out of it as it progresses towards spirituality and reaches the later goal of mankind. Thus in the future there will not only be the animal forms which are the incarnated images of human passion, but there will also be a race in which will live what man now hides within him as a portion of evil.[17]

This division into man and animal was necessary for the evolution of humanity.

Each animal form which separated in bygone times from the general stream signifies that man had then progressed a step further. . . .

Then follows a powerful description of how humanity is to evolve further, to overcome its own capacity for evil:

Through man having cast out of his line of development these animal forms – his elder brothers, as it were – he has reached his present height. Thus man rises by throwing out the lower forms in order to purify himself and he will rise still higher by separating out another kingdom of nature, the kingdom of the evil race. Thus mankind rises upward. Man owes

every quality he now possesses to the circumstance that he has rejected a
particular animal forms. One who with spiritual vision looks upon the
various animals knows exactly what we owe to each one of them. We look
upon the lion form and say: If the lion did not exist in the outer world,
man would not have had this or that quality; for through his having
rejected the lion he has acquired this or that quality. – This is the case
too with all the other forms in the animal kingdom.[18]

So not only are we teaching the children about the animals, and the relationship of the animals now on earth to the encompassing three-fold nature of the human being, we are also informing them, implicitly, of an even greater interdependence. Without the sacrifice of the animals, humanity would still be at the animal stage, would not yet have access to its own ego, would not have been ready for the Christ Impulse. "It was the mission of the Christ to give to human beings what they needed in order that they might feel themselves secure and firm within their separate individual egos."[19]

The Waldorf curriculum, no matter what the particular subject, sprouts from out of profound roots. Let us look briefly at another fourth grade topic: the Norse myths. In his book *Christianity As Mystical Fact*, Rudolf Steiner traces myths and sagas of Egypt and Greece to the Christ Impulse, and shows how these myths are picture of spiritual realities. For the fourth grade teacher, the following references are particularly illuminating:

When we go back to the distant past by studying the sagas and
myths, allowing the teaching of the Germanic gods to affect us, we find
communications from spiritual worlds arrayed in pictures. Such
communications are not, as academic scholarship would have us believe,
contrived images or personifications created by the folk imagination;
rather, they are real memories of those ancient days when people themselves
still knew what they had experienced. The sagas of Wotan, Thor, and so
on are such memories.[20]

And again:

> *It is a dreary arid learning with no inkling of real spiritual processes that asserts that all the figures of Nordic or Germanic mythology, of Greek mythology, all the record of gods and their deeds, are merely inventions of popular fantasy. . . . Everything in the old sagas and stories of the gods is the last relic, the last memory of pre-religious consciousness. The lore has remained of what men themselves have seen. Those who described Wotan, Thor, Zeus and so on, did so because they remembered that such things had been experienced once upon a time. Mythologies are fragments, broken pieces of what has once been experienced.[21]*

And most succinctly:

> *The one stream, more in the North, passed across Central Europe and bore the Christ as a Sun Hero, whether the name were Baldur or some other.[22]*

When we come to **fifth grade**, and our curriculum finds *terra firma* in both the sciences and the humanities, the expanding curriculum offers a plethora of examples. Let's start with botany. Much can be gleaned from Rudolf Steiner's many uses of the life cycle of the plant as analogy, as in the concluding words to his lecture of March 6, 1911:

> Theosophy is the bud for which the soul is the fertile ground, and morality is the blossom and fruit of the growing human/plant. [*Die Theosophie ist der Keim, die Seele ist der Fruchtboden für sie, und Moral ist Blüte und Frucht an der Pflanze des werdenden Menschen.*][23]

Such an analogy usually sheds light on both parts of the comparison.

Here is another:

The Word, which sounds forth from the soul, the Logos, was there in the beginning and so guided evolution that at last a being came into existence, in whom it also could manifest. What finally appears in time and space was already there in spirit from the beginning.

In order that this may be quite clear, let us make the following analogy. I have here a flower before me. This corolla, these petals, what were they a short time ago? A little seed. And in the seed, this white flower existed in potentiality. Were it not there potentially, this flower could not have come into existence. And whence comes the seed? It springs again from just such a flower. The blossom precedes the seed or fruit and again in like manner, the seed, from which this blossom has sprung, has been evolved out of a similar plant.... When we go back in human evolution we meet an imperfect human being and the significance of evolution is, that finally the Logos or Word which discloses the depths of the human soul may appear as its flower.[24]

But beyond analogy the anthroposophical descriptions of the plant world are almost always rooted, as it were, in evolution. For, like the animals of the fourth grade curriculum, which share the physical, etheric, and astral realms with the human being, the plants also are intimately related to human evolution. Following is a beautiful summation of that plant stage, which humanity left behind long ago.

We find the green color externally in the plant world, which covers the Earth with its mantel. And what is the human being's relationship to the plant? We know that humankind's existence on Saturn corresponds in a certain way to our minerals. Not that humankind was ever a mineral! Our present-day mineral kingdom is actually the youngest of the kingdoms of nature. We know, furthermore, that humankind led a plant-like existence on the Sun. Today a greenish sap flows in the plants. A similar fluid flowed in the human beings of that time. If, by magic, we could force astral components into the plant today, it would turn red! Because human beings received their astral body on the Moon, their inner fluid turned red – changed into red blood.

*Just reflect: the plant is chaste, it has no desires or passions—anger, fear, dread. Through the fact that people in a certain way became baser than the plant, they received into themselves something that raised them above the plant: the alert, ordinary consciousness. The plant world of today is sleeping. A plant is the upside-down human being. With its roots it points to the center of the Earth, where its I can be found. Exactly the same force that works downward in the plant, works just the opposite way upward in human beings. The fact that blood was acquired by human beings expresses the taking up of the I.[25] [Given in context of meditations enabling progress toward "the Christian principle. . . . You will rise again with your **glorified body**. . . . released from egoism. . . ."]*

The Rose Cross Meditation (see Steiner's book *Esoteric Science*) bids us dwell on just this relationship. In his lecture of February 16, 1907, entitled, "Who Are the Rosicrucians?"[26] Rudolf Steiner speaks about analogy. Somewhat stunningly he says, "Each person experiences an image of eternity in everything." And he then goes on to say that in the Rosicrucian schools of the Middle Ages, "the teacher said to the student, 'Consider the plant, how it sinks its roots into the ground and turns its blossom, the location of the reproductive organs upward to face the Sun. The blossoming calyx is kissed by a ray of sunlight, and thus a new being arises. The ray of sunlight is also called the holy lance of love.'"

Of course the Waldorf teacher must find a way to transform this explicit description into the right mood. The teacher's dwelling on such a Rosicrucian image can help to bring that mood about. For the botany in fifth grade is not yet the botany of the high school. Of course there must be enough science in the lessons to satisfy the fifth graders' growing capacities, but wonder is still the key to learning here. And such an image, as Rudolf Steiner bids us contemplate, will work wonders for us.

Greece has already been mentioned in relation to myths of the fourth grade. In the fifth grade, our understanding of the curriculum and its relationship to the child can be quickened when we realize that there is an inherent relationship between the "green mantel" of the plant world as a beautiful balance of the above with the below, and the harmony of ancient Greece. Science and art and religion were still harmoniously integrated at the time of the ancient Greeks. Beauty and science must be equally present for the fifth grader. Human beings and the gods share much. The Greek myths reflect the human being waking up to himself. For Rudolf Steiner's explication of many of the Greek myths, see: "The Greek Sages Before Plato in the Light of Mystery Wisdom," "The Wisdom of the Mysteries and the Myth," in *Christianity as Mystical Fact.* Or read any lecture on the fourth post Atlantean epoch.

In fifth grade we also encounter Buddha. His relationship to the Christ Impulse was mentioned in relation to the second grade curriculum and Francis of Assisi. For preparation of his appearance in the fifth grade curriculum we can turn to various lecture cycles including *The Gospel of St. Luke, From Buddha to Christ,* and *The Spiritual Guidance of Man and Mankind.*

Roman History – and with it the birth of Jesus of Nazareth, his Baptism and the incarnation of the Christ Impulse, as well as His Crucifixion – is studied in the **sixth grade**. By now history is the story of human beings, no longer the story of gods. That is the irony. The "turning point of time" takes place in the curriculum when the children's needs have become the visible world, the material world, the measurable, documented world. But the mood in which we tell the story of birth of the Christ child will be palpably different if we are inwardly aware of the monumentality of our story. Here is a marvelously succinct explanation of the timing of the Christ Event in human history:

> *Between the Atlantean Flood and the great War of All against All, man has had to renounce for a time the power to see into the spiritual world. He has had to content himself with seeing only what is around*

him in the physical world in so-called waking consciousness. This is now the normal condition. But in its place it has become possible for him fully to develop his consciousness of self, his individual ego. . . . This he has won. . . . But this ascent would not be possible if he had not taken part in that great cosmic event in the middle of our epoch. . . . Man would have been obliged to sink down into a kind of abyss had he not been preserved from it by the entry of Christ into our world. Let us represent the physical plane by this line; above it what is called the spiritual, the heavenly world, and below it what is called the abyss. Man really reaches the line separating the spiritual world from the abyss in the fourth age. . . . He now comes down and reaches the line during the period of the Roman Empire. . . That was at the time when the Roman idea of justice came into the world, when everyone's aim was to be a separate personality, an individual citizen. Man had then reached the line. At this point it was possible either to return or sink below it.[27]

Lest we think that Roman History offers the only congruency with our theme, let's remember that the optics main lesson is about light. And light, as we saw at the outset, is special:

First there was the Logos which became Life, then Light. . . . Into the human inner being, into the darkness, into the ignorance, the Light shone.[28]

Sprung from solar powers,
shining, world-blessing powers of spirit:
divine thinking has predestined you
to be Michaël's coat of rays.[29]

The obvious candidate to represent our theme in the **seventh grade** is the Renaissance – specifically, the three great artists Leonardo, Michelangelo, and Raphael. And, indeed, we would be derelict if we did not refer to Rudolf Steiner's revelation about Raphael, that he was the reincarnated Lazarus/John.[30] However, rather than dwell on these marvelous artists and Rudolf Steiner's many references to their achievements, let us take less likely subjects: physics, chemistry, physiology.

Seventh grade physics includes the mechanics of simple machines. World-class physicists, from Archimedes to Einstein and beyond, have always been merely a thin membrane removed from penetrating into the spiritual world. Such is their grasp of matter that they often realize, even if they cannot explain, Rudolf Steiner's indication that matter is spirit. When we grasp that inertia, gravity, levity, and force are all words that relate both to laws of physics and to the human soul, we realize how thin is the margin between this world and the next. The reference that follows takes the concept of "center of gravity" and applies it to world evolution. In a wonderful way, it illustrates the theme of the seventh grade, though astronomy, mathematics, and geometry also provide fruitful topics for further exploration. Rudolf Steiner himself "found" the spiritual world through geometry, as his autobiography makes clear. Here, then, the relevant excerpt:

> *Every system has only one center of gravity, every scale only one fulcrum. . . . That is why occultists in all times, in ancient as well as more recent times, when talking about the center of gravity of earth evolution in the true sense, indicate the one point in earth evolution, the Mystery of Golgotha, and the arising of human evolution again from this point onward. [Deshalb anerkennen die Okkultisten aller Zeiten, des Altertums und der Neuzeit, wenn von dem Schwerpunkt der Erdenevolution im wahren Sinne die Rede ist, dieses Hinwenden der Evolution zu dem einen Punkt, zu dem Mysterium von Golgatha, und das Aufsteigen der Menschheitsentwickelung wieder von diesem Punkte aus.]*[31]

Seventh grade chemistry deals with combustion and the limestone cycle. Fire, warmth, light. . . the sun. Again, the connection is apparent. The esoteric aspect of the limestone cycle is less self-evident:

> *When spring approaches. . . . the growing plants draw water and carbonic acid from the limestone in the soil. But this very loss signifies for the limestone an inner access of living activity, and it acquires on this account an extraordinary power of attraction for the Ahrimanic beings.*

Whenever spring approaches, their hopes revive. Apart from this, they have nothing particular to hope for from the realm of outer nature, because they are really able to pursue their activities only within human beings. But when spring draws near, the impression which the spring-limestone makes on them gives them the idea that after all they will be able to spread their dragon-nature through nature at large. (44) [...] If they were to succeed... then, in autumn, the Earth would feel pain at every footfall on its surface. ...

Just as the Ahrimanic beings nourish their hopes and experience their illusions down below, so the Luciferic beings experience their hopes and illusions up above.... When now in spring the plants begin to sprout, they draw in and assimilate carbon dioxide... it rises into the realm of the plants, and there it is drawn towards the Luciferic beings. While the Ahrimanic beings strive to ensoul the living limestone with a kind of astral rain, the Luciferic beings try to raise up a sort of carbon dioxide mist or vapor from the Earth. If they were to succeed, human beings on Earth would no longer be able to breathe.... If the Ahrimanic beings could realize their hopes, the whole of humanity would gradually be dissolved into the earth.... (46)

Although the Mystery of Golgotha had indeed to enter as a once-for-all event into the history of the Earth, it is in a sense renewed for human beings every year. We can learn to feel how the Luciferic force up above would like to suffocate physical humanity in carbon dioxide vapor, while down below, the Ahrimanic forces would like to vivify the limestone masses of the Earth with an astral rain, so that man himself would be calcified and reduced to limestone. But then, for a person who can see into these things, there arises between the Luciferic and the Ahrimanic forces the figure of Christ. (51)[32]

This is an entirely transcendent perspective on the usual litmus test experiment of seventh grade chemistry.

Turning our attention to biology, we can perhaps sum up with this quotation the mood in which we need to conduct the teaching of human physiology in the seventh grade:

> *And those who believe that man is merely the apparatus of bones,*
> *blood, flesh and so forth, of which natural science, physiology, biology and*
> *anatomy speak, have no understanding of his nature.[33]*

More specifically, Rudolf Steiner refers in various lectures to the miracle of the femur:

> *Take, for example, a piece of the thigh-bone and you will see that it is*
> *not composed of a solid mass, but it is a fine interweaving of supports*
> *which are arranged into a marvelous structure. And if we seek to discover*
> *the law upon which this bone is constructed, we find that it follows the*
> *law which develops the greatest strength with the least expenditure of*
> *material in order to be able to support the upper part of the human body.*
> *Our engineering art is not yet so far advanced that it can build such a*
> *highly artistic structure as the all over-ruling wisdom has fashioned.*
> *Mankind will not possess such wisdom until later in its evolution. Divine*
> *wisdom pervades the whole of nature;* human *wisdom will only gradually*
> *reach this height.[34]*

This description of the thigh bone comes in the context of spiritual scientific insights concerning the evolution from the moon, as the cosmos of wisdom, to the earth as the cosmos of love. Wisdom, which was prepared on the moon, now manifests in the thigh bone (to name that one example); love will be prepared on the earth and will come to be manifest in the future. The uniting of wisdom with love is the mission of the Christ Impulse.

Elsewhere, Rudolf Steiner refers to the thigh bone as a "masterpiece of natural architecture."[35] And again:

> *We have often pointed to the miraculous wisdom found in the*
> *structure of even a little piece of thigh-bone! It does not consist of a*
> *compact mass, but of many delicate lattice-like structures which are so*
> *wonderfully put together that the greatest carrying capacity is attained*
> *with the expenditure of the smallest amount of matter, such as no engineer*
> *of the present day can achieve.[36]*

Here is Rudolf Steiner himself filled with wonder. And wonder is a mood which benefits seventh graders. That is why the block called "Wish, Wonder, and Surprise" forms part of the seventh grade curriculum.[37] But wonder, like the thigh bone or the "bones, blood, flesh, and so forth, of which natural science, physiology, biology, and anatomy speak" as well as combustion and the limestone cycle, can all provide us with deep wellsprings of wonder, the wonder that spreads warmth and reminds us of Alpha and Omega.

Although the **eighth grade** curriculum could also be culled for subject-specific allusions to our theme, let us look at an overall indication for this grade level. We are to bring the children to the present day. The last day of eighth grade history should end with that day's morning newspaper. A tall order! But an equally daunting task is to find ideals of human behavior, impressive biographies of nobility, of sacrifice, of courage – in short, biographies that reveal something of a Michaëlic impulse, something of the Christ Impulse in human history.

Sometimes I suggest that teacher training students who think they might one day be eighth grade teachers start a notebook of possible biographies, or biographical incidents, such as can be found in newspapers and other media. There are the obvious examples: Gandhi, Martin Luther King, Rosa Parks. But there are less obvious examples: stories of ordinary people who, when disaster strikes, do not think first and foremost of themselves. Such stories should never be cranked up, sentimentalized, or toned down for the youngsters. It takes perseverance to find the Rosicrucian heroes of our day. But they do exist, and it is a significant path of research to discover them. Through them the Christ Impulse lives, providing an antidote to the carnage of modern warfare, which is also part of the eighth grade curriculum.

By now it should be clear that once recognized as a revealed secret, the Christ Impulse becomes ubiquitous in the Waldorf curriculum.

Arriving at the **high school**, we find that the curriculum raises our theme from the substratum, where the teacher alone is aware of it, to the level where students themselves can engage with it. Of course, such awareness grows in comprehension as we move up through the grades. Let us consider some of the likely platforms. [My own area being literature, I will stay within that context, but parallels in the sciences have already been alluded to in the discussion of seventh grade and can, most definitely, be traced through the high school science curriculum.]

In the **ninth grade** there is history of art. Unavoidably, the subject of the life of Christ comes up. Why did the great painters all choose this theme for their paintings? Were they unable to think of other subjects? Why, for that matter, did so many great musicians also choose this theme? (Of course, that would be a question for the 11th grade History Through Music class.) In the context of Giotto and the Renaissance painters, one can have marvelous conversations with ninth graders. The paintings provide the mood if the teacher can first get the students to observe carefully, "scientifically," the technical ingredients, such as composition, distribution of dark and light, and balance, before turning the conversation to the content, the story depicted in the painting. By the time the main lesson has moved to Turner or even Van Gogh and their attention to light and sun, one can find the connection to the works and the intentions of the earlier masters. The relationship between the halos in the earlier works, and the fascination with sunlight in the later works, can be explored. Now that we are in high school, we can talk about light and sun as metaphors, as poetic realities. Generally, ninth graders are not yet interested in deeper philosophical or theological aspects. Nor should we burden them with these considerations. But in the presence of a masterpiece by, say, Raphael or Rembrandt, ninth graders can be touched to the quick in spite of themselves.

Another example of a reference to our theme can be found in connection to the ninth grade Comedy and Tragedy main lesson. In explaining "the first sign" of Christ at the Marriage in Cana, Rudolf Steiner mentions Dionysus. Though any conventional history of drama will mention Dionysus – for instance, "The Greek drama began as a religious observance in honor of Dionysus"[38] – Rudolf Steiner gives us the esoteric background of Dionysus in the context of explaining why Christ chose Cana in Galilee, and why wine was involved for this first miracle:

> *Alcohol has the effect of severing the connection of the human being with the spirit world in which he previously existed. It still has this effect today. It was not without reason that alcohol has had a place in human evolution. In the future of humanity, it will be possible to see in the fullest sense of the word that it was the mission of alcohol to draw men so deeply into materiality that they become egoistic, thus bringing them to the point of claiming the ego for themselves, no longer placing it at the service of the whole folk. Alcohol performed a service, the contrary of the one performed by the human group-soul. It deprived men of the capacity to feel themselves at one with the whole in the spirit world.* **Hence the Dionysian worship which cultivated a living together in a kind of external intoxication, a merging into the whole without observing this whole.** *Evolution in the post-Atlantean period has been connected with the worship of Dionysus, because this worship was a symbol of the function and mission of alcohol. . . . In the same period in which men were drawn most deeply into egotism through alcohol, there appeared a force stronger than all others which could give to them the greatest impulse for re-finding a union with the spiritual whole. On the one hand men had to descend to the lowest level in order that they might become independent, and on the other hand a strong force must come which can give again the impulse for finding the path back to the Universal. The Christ indicated this to be His mission in the first of His signs.*[39] (Emphasis added)

That intoxication was part of the cult of Dionysus is one aspect, that the cult of Dionysus had a mission in world evolution is the greater context, and that the "strong force must come which can give again the impulse for finding the path back to the Universal" is the core. How much of this can or should be part of the lesson must be left to the individual choice of the teacher. For the youngsters, it is more a matter of mood than content, but the teacher's awareness of this background will surely find its way to the students.

In **tenth grade**, we have the history of the word, or Word, and its inherent relation to Logos. We cannot really deal with the history of literature without reference to the beginning of the Gospel of St. John, and although we may ask the students to speak those words in a speech chorus as an example of powerful verse, we should not expect of them any natural inclinations toward profundity. But for the teachers, any of Rudolf Steiner's many explications will provide illumination, for as we have already seen, "Everything is an incarnation of the Logos."[40]

> *For even as early as the Saturn period this physical human body was directed in such a way that it later became capable of speech, became a witness of the Logos. That you are formed as you are today, that this human body has its present shape, rests upon the fact that the "Word" lies at the very foundation of the whole plan of our creation.*[41]

In the earlier consideration of the alphabet as it relates to the first grade, we have already met the awesome descriptions of Alpha and Omega, of Elders and Angels. Here is another example of the occult history of language:

> *We express what we want to say in language, which is to bring out what lives in our souls. The expression of soul content in language differs from one epoch of human development to another. In the Hebraic epoch, the ancient Hebrew sacred language provided a wonderful way of expressing things. It was very different from our way of clothing the*

secrets of the soul into words. When a word was spoken in old Hebrew, it contained not merely an abstract idea, as it does today, but a whole world. The vowels were not written because the speaker expressed his innermost being through his way of vocalizing, whereas the consonants contained the description – the picture, so to speak – of what was outside.

Specifically:

When the Hebrews wrote, for example, what corresponds to our B, they always felt something like a picture of outer conditions, something that formed a warm, hut-like enclosure. The letter B always evoked the image of something that can enclose a being like a house; the letter could not be pronounced without this image living in the speaker's soul. When A was vocalized, there was always something of strength and force, even of radiating power, living within it. . . . Obviously, language was then a far more living affair.[42]

Rudolf Steiner goes on to consider the contemporary situation: "Our language expresses only abstractions and generalities, and we no longer even notice this. . . " Tenth graders, weaned on the dead language of commercialism and the media, will be able to enter into this discussion. The clincher, the end of that sentence, says ". . . so our language at bottom expresses only the philistine." Here is a marvelous opportunity for a "teaching moment." What does "philistine" mean, and why would it be used in this context? I do not advocate quoting Rudolf Steiner. Rather, it is a matter of getting at Rudolf Steiner's thoughts about the quality of language, an intensely contemporary issue. This main lesson provides an opportunity for considering just such questions. Rudolf Steiner continues:

It could not be otherwise in an age when people begin to write literature long before they have any spiritual content to express, when an infinite amount of printed material goes to the general public, when everyone thinks he must write something, and when everything can be a subject to write about.

Here is another wonderful springboard for a consideration of
the world in which our tenth graders live.

Before leaving this theme, let us look at a reference taken from
a pedagogical lecture cycle. In a talk about eurythmy, Rudolf
Steiner describes the Logos in the context of historical Greece:

> *In Greece there was still quite a different feeling. . . . There was a
> tingling, an urge in the human being to let the will reveal itself through
> the limbs, with every syllable, with every word, every phrase, with the
> rhythm and measure of every phrase. . . . Words were to him expressions
> for the forces of cloud formation, the forces lying in the growth of plants
> and all natural phenomena. The word rumbled in the rolling waves, worked
> in the whistling wind. Just as the word lives in my breath so that I make
> a corresponding movement, so did the Greek find all that was living in
> the word in the raging wind, in the surging wave, even in the rumbling
> earthquake. These were words pouring out of the earth.*
>
> *Our words have become intellectualistic; they no longer have creative
> power. . . . Greek gymnastics was a revelation of the Word. . . . The Word
> worked in Greek wrestling. The shadowy image of the Word in music
> worked in the Greek Dances.*
>
> *We must realize how feeble our ideas have become in modern
> civilization, and come to perceive rightly how the mighty impulse pulsating
> through such a line as "in the Beginning was the Word" was weakened
> when it passed over into Roman culture, becoming more and more shadowy,
> until all we now feel is an inner lassitude when we speak it.*[43]

From Rome we pass to the Middle Ages, where, according to
Rudolf Steiner, the Logos became "the dead Logos."

> *Only the dead Logos could be tolerated in man. And those who were
> educated were not only educated by having the dead Logos communicated
> to them, but also the dead word — the Latin tongue in its decay. The
> dying word of speech became the chief medium of education up to the
> time of the sixteenth century, when there arose a certain inner revolt
> against it.*

The lecture ends with a plea for re-enlivening the Logos. This tenth grade main lesson – called variously History of Language, History Through Language, Epic, Poetics, or the like – can have the life-long result of revivifying the students' relationship to Logos.

As we reach the upper half of high school, we find that our theme has become an explicit part of the curriculum. We cannot teach Parsifal in the **eleventh grade** without reference to the Holy Grail and what it represents. In lecture V of a lecture cycle concerning the story of Parsifal,[44] Rudolf Steiner also reveals his own method of occult research. In the context of Parsifal's quest, Rudolf Steiner describes his own quest, over the course of many years, to comprehend the occult significance of "the Parsifal secret, the secret of the Holy Grail."[45] It is an unusual laying bare, in the opus of Rudolf Steiner, of his own process of research, and it comes in the context of laying bare the occult nature of the Christ Impulse:

> *The Christ Impulse does not work where there is strife, but below the surface, and human wisdom will have to uncover a great deal that we may think strange, if we look at it superficially. Much will have to be revealed as a symptom of the Christ Impulse working below the surface.*[46]

So, in the context of the hidden Christ Impulse, Rudolf Steiner traces the surfacing, in his own understanding, of the relationship of Parsifal, the seeker, to the Holy Grail. The following words by Rudolf Steiner are as apt for Parsifal's story as they are for Rudolf Steiner's commentary on his own search:

> *In occult researches of this kind one is often held back, delayed, so that one may not do too much in a day or a year and be driven on to speculate about the truth. Landmarks appear. For me they appeared in the course of really a good many years, during which I sought an answer to the question – Where will you find the name of Parsifal written on the Holy Grail?*[47]

Can there be any question that an eleventh grade teacher who has had the good fortune to study this pertinent lecture cycle by Rudolf Steiner will stand before the questing eleventh graders with a far broader scope of understanding than one who has not? For one thing, our own modest attempts at research into the material we are presenting to our students through the curriculum can find many levels of support here: the support of Rudolf Steiner's research revealed; the support of Rudolf Steiner's explication of Parsifal; the support of recognizing the occult nature of the Christ Impulse, i.e., knowing that that *is* what we are working with. And of course, the young people we are teaching do not want to be held back. All the more reason to show them that Parsifal's growth had to be delayed, if truth was to be his.

A less obvious but no less compelling literary illustration of our theme arises through the romantic poets (whether taught in tenth or eleventh grade). In his book, *Romanticism Comes of Age*, Owen Barfield traces the path from romanticism to anthroposophy. In a word, what these paths have in common is an understanding of the relationship between microcosm and macrocosm. In a word, the romantic poets clothe this understanding in pictures. Theirs is a truly penetrating imagination. Can the literature teacher discern in the brilliant lyrics and vibrant language of Shelley and Keats, in the ambitious evocations of Wordsworth and Coleridge, "the Christ Impulse working below the surface"? It is not so very far beneath the surface of their works, hidden though it may have been from their own self-consciousness. Secular in their life-styles though these poets were, they drew their inspiration from Logos-consciousness. Perhaps it is no exaggeration to say that language was their religion and imagination was their priest.[48] They were forerunners.

> *The genuine spiritual-scientific attitude is to restore in us the faculty of seeing in nature not the ghost-like things of which science speaks, but the pictorial, the imaginative.*[49]

For a comprehensive guide to our theme, the teacher of literature will be greatly aided by Christy MacKaye Barnes' *For the Love of Literature: A Celebration of Language and Imagination.*[50] As this collection of essays makes clear, the teacher's approach to the lofty must, like the romantic poets' approach to their own themes (nature, imagination, individuality, transcendence), be couched in rigor, structure, and discipline. The romantics did not oppose form. They espoused it. Their sonnets were strict. "Scorn not the sonnet," wrote Wordsworth in a sonnet; " . . . the sonnet sweet," wrote Keats in "On the Sonnet." Through the transparent structures of their poetry, they evoked great passion, great beauty, and great truth. They soared on the "viewless wings of Poesy," to the heights of Logos.

Even when our curriculum raises the Christ Impulse into plain view, we must be pictorial or, as Emerson would say, emblematic. And Emerson brings us to the **twelfth grade,** when the study of Emerson and the Transcendentalists, or of Goethe's *Faust,* or of Tolstoy and Dostoevsky all provide ample scope for different facets of the impulse we have been tracing. The transformation of evil, the nature of suffering and of forgiveness, compassion and the story teller's allegories for these themes – these now become the stuff of twelfth grade curriculum. Twelfth graders are capable of applying their own individualizing thinking to the thoughts of Emerson, the questions of Dostoevsky, the images of *Faust.* They can write their own parables.

Let us end by considering a transcendentalist, and therefore a twelfth grade, theme: analogy. Rudolf Steiner says: "One acquires Imagination by seeing an emblem in every thing."[51] Emerson makes a similar remark in his essay on Nature: "Nature is the symbol of spirit." Or in the words of one of Emerson's biographers: "Emerson moves from the proposition that 'words are signs of natural fact,' to the further proposition that 'particular natural facts are symbols of particular spiritual facts.'"[52]

Here is a fuller explication of what Rudolf Steiner meant:

> *We may not yet have access to the world of Imagination, but it is a world that is attainable. We must develop soul forces that are objective, comparable to the forces active in our eyes. We would be surrounded by perpetual darkness if the eyes did not transform the light falling upon them into coloured images and mental pictures. Anyone who believes we must just wait for some nebulous manifestation of the spirit to appear has no comprehension of the inner work required of human beings. The soul must become active, as the eyes are active transforming light. Unless the soul creates pictures and images within itself, the spiritual world cannot stream in. The pictures thus created will maintain objectivity provided they are not prompted by egoistic wishes; when their content is spiritual, then healing forces stream into a person's soul. **When the ability to transform the concepts of spiritual science into vivid pictures full of colour, sound, and life is attained, when the whole world becomes such a picture, then this wisdom becomes in all spheres of life a healing force, not only for ourselves but for others, for the whole world.*** [Emphasis added][53]

There is our challenge. Can each individual teacher transform the Waldorf curriculum, which is emblematic in nature, into the personally found, objective pictures which are true to what we are teaching, and thus true to anthroposophy, which is to say true to the Christ Impulse?

> *Truly, like a stream which has disappeared into mountain cavities, so that it is no longer to be seen up above. . . the Christ Impulse works on below the surface – works . . . as occult, i.e. hidden, reality.[54]*

It is this hidden reality that truly educates our children.

"The teacher," says Rudolf Steiner, "must again come to an understanding of the Word." For, to repeat, "Everything is an incarnation of the Logos."

> *With this supersensible within the sensible, with this rediscovery of the spirit which has been lost in the Word, in the Logos, since the Word became an idol, with this rediscovery of the spirit begins the new era of education.... What we have to find to-day ... are the means which will lead us to reality.*[55]

"...the means which will lead us to reality" is the consciousness we bring to bear on the hidden reality working below the surface of our curriculum.

> *For no education will develop from abstract principles or programs — it will only develop from reality. And because man himself is soul and spirit, because he has a physical nature, a soul nature and a spiritual nature, reality must again come into our life — for with the whole reality will the spirit also come into our life, and only such a spirit as this can sustain the educational art of the future.*

This is a mighty and magnificent task, the task of providing the chariot for Michaël:

> *Michaël needs, as it were, a chariot by means of which to enter our civilization.... By educating in the right way, we are preparing Michaël's chariot for his entrance into our civilization.*[56]

References

[1] *Encyclopedia Britannica.*

[2] "The Last Address" (Dornach: 28 September 1924), in *The Archangel Michaël: His Mission and Ours*, selected lectures and writings by Rudolf Steiner (Hudson, NY: Anthroposophic Press, 1994), p. 283.

[3] Rudolf Steiner, GA 103 (Hamburg: May 1908), *The Gospel of St. John* (New York: Anthroposophic Press, 1940), Lecture 3, p.50.

[4] Ibid.

[5] Ibid., p. 54.

[6] GA 211, *Das Sonnenmysterium und das Mysterium von Tod und*

Aufstehung, p. 216.

[7] Rudolf Steiner, *The Younger Generation* (Spring Valley, NY: Anthroposophic Press, 1967), p. 174.

[8] GA 346 (Dornach: September 1924), *The Book of Revelation and the Work of the Priest,* Lecture 3, p. 45.

[9] Ibid., Lecture 6, p. 83.

[10] GA 155 (Norrköping, Sweden: 28-30 May 1912), *The Spiritual Foundation of Morality; Francis of Assisi and the Mission of Love,* pp. 43, 45-47.

[11] GA 109, "Principles of Spiritual Economy", in *From Buddha to Christ,* (New York: Anthroposophic Press, 1978), p. 21.

[12] GA 149, *Christ and the Spiritual World,* p. 84.

[13] GA 103, *The Gospel of St. John,* Lecture 3, p. 52.

[14] GA 346, *The Book of Revelation,* Lecture 9, p. 129.

[15] GA 112 (Kassel: June-July 1909), *The Gospel of St. John and Its Relation to the Other Gospels,* especially Lecture 8.

[16] GA 8, *Christianity as Mystical Fact* (New York: Anthroposophic Press, 1947/1972), Chapter 9, p. 151.

[17] GA 104 (Nuremberg: June 1908), *The Apocalypse of St. John* (New York: Anthroposophic Press, 1992), Lecture 4, p. 80.

[18] Ibid., p. 82.

[19] GA 103, *The Gospel of St. John,* p. 69.

[20] GA 102, "Christianity Began as a Religion but is Greater than All Religions," in *The Christian Mystery* (New York: Anthroposophic Press, 1998), p. 275.

[21] GA 104, *The Apocalypse of St. John,* p. 17.

[22] Rudolf Steiner, *Karmic Relations,* Volume VIII, Chapter 6, p. 81.

[23] GA 127.

[24] GA 103, *The Gospel of St. John,* p. 27.

[25] GA 264, *From the History and Contents of the First Section of the Esoteric School, 1904-1914* (New York: Anthroposophic Press,1998), p.187.

[26] GA 97.

[27] GA 104, *The Apocalypse of St. John,* p. 121.

[28] GA 103, *The Gospel of St. John,* p. 41.

[29] "The Last Address", p. 284.

[30] See "The Last Address" (the latter part of this address is not included in the excerpt given in *The Archangel Michael*). See

also *Eternal Individuality* by Sergei Prokofieff.

[31] GA 127 (5 June 1911), p. 177 [passage from the lecture translated by the author].

[32] GA 229, "The Easter Imagination" (7 October 1923), in *The Four Seasons and the Archangels* (London: Rudolf Steiner Press, 1984), pp. 44, 46.

[33] GA 182 (Zürich: 1918), *The Work of the Angels in Man's Astral Body*, p. 9.

[34] GA 103, *The Gospel of St. John*, Lecture 3, p. 47.

[35] Rudolf Steiner, *Cosmic Memory, Prehistory of Earth and Man* (W. Nyack: Rudolf Steiner Publications, 1959), pp. 226-227.

[36] GA 104, *The Apocalypse of St. John*, Lecture 7, p. 126.

[37] For further references to wonder (as well as wish and surprise), see "The Art and Science of Teaching Composition," by Dorit Winter (Fair Oaks, CA: AWSNA Publications, 1998).

[38] http://www.watson.org/~leigh/drama.html.

[39] GA 103, *The Gospel of St. John*, pp. 85-86.

[40] Ibid., p. 50.

[41] Ibid., p.39.

[42] Rudolf Steiner, *The Universal Human*, pp. 52-53.

[43] GA 307 (August 1923, "Ilkley Course"), *Education and Modern Spiritual Life*, Lecture 5, pp. 98-99.

[44] See GA 149 (Leipzig: 28 December 1913 – 2 January 1914), *Christ and the Spiritual World and the Search for the Holy Grail*.

[45] Ibid., p. 111.

[46] Ibid., p. 95.

[47] Ibid., p. 98.

[48] For further discussion of Coleridge and his relationship to Truth and spiritual science, see "Glimmers of Truth," by Dorit Winter in *The Golden Blade*, 2000.

[49] See Rudolf Steiner, *Education as a Social Problem*, Chapter 3.

[50] Hudson, New York: Anthroposophic Press, 1996.

[51] Rudolf Steiner (16 February 1907), *Das Christliche Mysterium*.

[52] Robert D. Richardson, *Emerson: The Mind on Fire* (Berkeley: University of California Press, 1995), p. 231.

[53] GA 55 (Berlin: 14 February 1907), "Wisdom and Health", in *Supersensible Knowledge* (Great Barrington, MA: Anthroposophic Press, 1987), p. 64. (The whole lecture can be found in *Isis*

Mary Sophia: Her Mission and Ours, selected lectures by Rudolf Steiner, edited by Christopher Bamford, SteinerBooks, 2003.)

54 GA 149, *Christ and the Spiritual World and the Search for the Holy Grail,* p. 97.

55 GA 307, *Education and Modern Spiritual Life,* p.104.

56 Rudolf Steiner, *The Younger Generation,* p.174 [emphasis added].

Amicus Curiae (Friend of the Court Brief) "Anthroposophy Is Not a Religion"

prepared by Douglas Sloan

[1.-11. are procedural points and not germane here. Ed.]

12. By all scholarly criteria of what constitutes religion, anthroposophy is not a religion.

13. On April 10, 2004, I provided an expert report containing my opinion that anthroposophy is not a religion under academic analysis and definition.

14. In considering the relation of anthroposophy to religion, I considered briefly some of the main approaches to the scholarly study of religion itself, in order to approach more precisely what can and cannot be said to constitute religion, and, more specifically, a religion.

15. The attempt to define religion has been notoriously difficult, and the approaches to doing so are many. In general there have been three main approaches.

16. The first can perhaps be called the essentialist approach. Essentialist definitions tend to focus on the inner essence or substance, the metaphysical reality claims, of religions, and the relationships to these demanded of human beings by the claimed realities. One of the conceptual difficulties with this focus is that philosophers and others can make metaphysical and ethical arguments about the nature of reality without advancing these as themselves constituting a religion, although they may well have implications for religion.

17. The second main approach to the study and definition of religion can be called the functional approach, and is probably the theoretical approach most favored by social scientists, although as I shall point out, some theologians also favor it. Functional definitions of religion stress the effects, the functions of religion, in actual life—the ways in which religion functions to fulfill basic human needs, both individually and communally. Different

scholars stress different functions as the defining characteristic of religion. Among these various functional definitions are, for examples: the cognitive–religion provides meaning systems for understanding and coping with life; the psychological–religion functions to meet psychological needs, such as, a sense of security in the face of life's uncertainties, a sense of identity, a sense of purpose, and so forth; the social–religion serves primarily to provide values for social cohesion and the preservation of the social group; and the ideological (Marxist definitions of religion are a good example)–religion serves the power interests of governing elites by deluding the masses. Each of these taken by itself is decidedly reductionist, and, in order to avoid inordinate reductionism, most scholars attempt to fashion combinations of various functional approaches.

18. One form of functionalism, often utilized by students of religion, is that of the twentieth-century American theologian, Paul Tillich. Religion Tillich defined as expressing "the ultimate concern" of an individual or of an entire culture. Every person and every society, he argued, has its "ultimate concern" (often, to be sure, directed toward less than ultimate objective realities). In fact, for Tillich, every culture is grounded in its own ultimate concern, to which it gives concrete expression. Culture itself as a whole is, therefore, the religious expression and activity par excellence. "Religion," Tillich famously wrote, "is the substance of culture, culture is the form of religion." (Tillich, 1959) Tillich's position can be a good illustration of how the strength of the functionalist can also be its main weakness. The strength is that it enables one to see the religious functions, as noted above, of many human activities not usually recognized as religious: the state, the university, science, technology, the stock exchange, Sunday afternoon football, and so on. Each has its ultimate concern, and often its own "priesthood," paths of initiation, dogmas, sacred texts, and other marks of religion. The weakness is that a definition which begins to apply to everything often ends up telling us little about anything.

19. In view of these various approaches, it is not surprising that one leading historian of American religion (Catherine Albanese of UC Santa Barbara), whose works I reviewed in forming my opinion, has observed that scholars have become increasingly less certain about what should be counted as religion as a general phenomenon. "In the end," she writes, "religion is a feature that encompasses all of human life, and therefore it is difficult if not impossible to define it." (*Albanese, America: Religions and Religion,* 1992, pp.2-3).

20. In this light it is probably also not surprising that historians of religion turn mainly to the third approach to the definition of religion, namely, the formal. Scholars in the history of religion and comparative religion deal primarily with the actual religious forms manifested by concrete religious groups and movements. These religious forms include such things as beliefs and doctrines (creeds), ritual activities, forms of worship, sacred texts, and recognized sources of authority. The advantage and strength of this approach is that it is concrete and makes it possible to determine whether a group actually functions, not just religiously in general, a la Paul Tillich, for instance, but as a formal, identifiable religion as such. It also is possible then to distinguish it in detail from other religions and their forms, and to trace the actual development of a specific religion over time. In this perspective, a religious group is one that manifests and is organized around these common religious forms, albeit with its own distinct versions of them. This approach can also incorporate aspects of the first two approaches.

21. It is especially from the perspective of this third approach to the definition of religion, the formal, that I can meaningfully and concretely testify that anthroposophy is not a religion.

22. My personal knowledge of anthroposophy stems from my involvement over the past sixteen (16) years with the Anthroposophic Press, the Anthroposophical Society of North America, and my relationship with Sunbridge College. I was on the Board of Directors of the Anthroposophic Press from 1988-

1996; I was president of the board of directors for the Association of Waldorf Schools of North America from 1993-1996; and I was also the director of the masters in Waldorf education program at Sunbridge College from 1992-2000.

23. The Austrian philosopher Rudolf Steiner was born in Austria in 1861 and died in Dornach, Switzerland in 1925.

24. Apart from a few lectures given in Scandinavia and Great Britain, Steiner's entire life and work were spent in Germany and Switzerland. All his lectures and books were presented originally in the German language. Many, though not all, of his books and lectures have been translated into various other languages, including English.

25. Anthroposophy is the name given by Rudolf Steiner to designate the way of knowing, the method of inquiry, that he established.

26. Perhaps a note about the term anthroposophy is in order. When first experienced by Americans the term frequently seems strange. However, as a moment's reflection can show, it need be no stranger than the wholly familiar word, anthropology, except that instead of the Greek word logos, commonly translated in this connection narrowly as "study," the Greek word for "wisdom," sophia, is joined to the Greek for human being, anthropos. What this "wisdom of the human being" might include Steiner attempted to show in considerable detail throughout his life (including some 6000 lectures that he gave in the course of his life). Because he maintained that all that he presented as anthroposophy was the result of a way of knowing, a mode of inquiry, every element in it is subject to being weighed and evaluated by each individual using his or her own freedom of judgment.

27. Steiner also frequently spoke of anthroposophy as "spiritual science." This is a literal English translation of the German word Geisteswissenschaft, the word used in the German university for what in English is termed the "Humanities." In the German university the natural sciences are called the Naturwissenschaften, and what we designate as the humanities are called the

Geisteswissenschaften–literally, "spiritual sciences." In the German university, therefore, the spiritual sciences include all those subjects having to do with meaning, value, and qualities. Literature, philosophy, history, and the arts, as well as theology, are all "spiritual sciences," Geisteswissenschaften. Steiner clearly wanted to deepen the Geisteswissenschaften and to put the realms of meaning, value, and qualities on a solid knowledge foundation (a need recognized by leading thinkers at the time), a foundation that would open new avenues of inquiry and that would ultimately have consequences not only for the traditional humanities but also for the natural sciences as well.

28. Accordingly, out of Steiner's work have come new movements in a variety of fields, among them movements in medicine, agriculture, the arts, mathematics, social thought and economics, education, and religion.

29. As stated above, Rudolf Steiner presented anthroposophy as a way of knowing, a method of inquiry. He set forth the epistemological ground for this way of knowing in his two earliest publications, his doctoral dissertation, *Truth and Knowledge*, published in 1892, and, following shortly thereafter in 1894, his book *The Philosophy of Freedom* (Steiner, 1963a; Steiner, 1964).

30. Rudolf Steiner considered *The Philosophy of Freedom* to be his most important work for it developed the foundations for anthroposophy as a way of knowing.

31. In *The Philosophy of Freedom* Steiner addressed what he saw as two interrelated questions, that of the nature of human knowing and that of the possibility of genuine human freedom of will grounded in knowing. In this book he attempted to show that human thinking, understood and developed in its depths, is unlimited in its possibilities, and can, therefore, be the basis for free and responsible human action, shorn of all biological, social, or creedal determinism. Thinking, he argued, has the potential of being able to deal with the qualitative realm–the realm of meaning, values, and qualities as such–just as rigorously as it now deals with the quantitative–that which we can count, measure, and weigh.

32. The human being, Steiner sought to show in these early works, has the possibility for genuine creativity and moral freedom and responsibility based on knowledge, not just on belief. These emphases—a way of knowing for exploring the many dimensions of the world, including especially the qualitative, and individual freedom of decision and action based on this way of knowing—have been from its beginning the central, guiding principles of anthroposophy.

33. Two further observations about Steiner's development of anthroposophy as a way of knowing might be helpful. First, while anthroposophy claims to open new methods and areas of knowledge, this does not mean that Steiner was unaware or unappreciative of other traditions of knowing, or that he saw no connection or continuity between his approach and those of many others. Steiner was fully aware of and saw himself in an appreciative-critical relationship with the whole western tradition of philosophy (Steiner, 1973), and was deeply knowledgeable of eastern thought. As a young man he was selected to edit the scientific papers of Johann Wolfgang von Goethe, and spent seven years at the task, producing what is considered by many to be the definitive edition of Goethe's scientific work. He subsequently again and again referred to Goethe's scientific method as a fundamental contact point for understanding and developing his own epistemological and scientific approach (Steiner, 1950; Steiner, 1968). The reappraisal, only recently now taking place, of Goethe's scientific work, long dismissed as unimportant, adds weighty support to Steiner's view of the significance of Goethe in this respect (Amrine, 1987; Seaman & Zajonc, 1998). Steiner also saw his epistemology as carrying forward the phenomenological and epistemological approach then being developed in Germany, and he dedicated his doctoral thesis to Eduard von Hartmann, one of the founders of modern phenomenology.

34. The second observation has to do with the breadth of Steiner's interests and activities. As is evident, Steiner addressed a variety of areas, not all of which are touched on here. He also was

not reticent in producing his own research findings to be considered a part of anthroposophy. In doing so, however, Steiner always insisted that every individual has to decide for him or herself what in the content he presented is convincing and what not. Nor did Steiner intend that what he said was the final or the whole word on a particular subject. It is significant, in my judgment, that a word frequently used by anthroposophists themselves to describe Steiner's information on a particular subject is the word, "indications," as in, "Steiner's indications about...." "Indications" suggests possible fruitful ideas to consider, activities to try out, subjects to contemplate, directions to pursue.

35. It is a wholly personal choice not only whether one follows Steiner's method of knowing and tries to develop it, but also whether, out of conviction, one accepts–or does not–Steiner's own results and content flowing from that method as he practiced it. If the principle of individual freedom based on knowledge is violated in following Steiner's indications, then the entire method is vitiated.

36. It is the case that Steiner ranged widely in many directions, and often in great detail. And in his lectures he presented his findings about science, education, economics, and so forth, but also his findings about the nature of the human being as body, soul, and spirit, the world of spirit, of life before and after death, even speaking at great length about beings such as the Christ, angels, archangels, and others.

37. Clearly much of what Steiner said had direct relevance for religion. Yet, this is true of many thinkers from, for examples, Plato and Aristotle to Spinoza and Leibniz, to William James and, in our own recent time, Alfred North Whitehead.

38. Whitehead, for instance, a great mathematician and logician, developed a philosophical system which included as central to it the concepts of God, immaterial creativity, and eternal objects.

39. Not surprisingly, religious thinkers of many sorts–Protestant, Catholic, Buddhist–have found Whitehead's philosophy congenial to their own religious interests, and have drawn on it extensively, even developing from Whitehead's so-called process

philosophy various versions of process theology.

40. Whitehead, however, was not propounding a religion but rather a philosophical approach based on his own inquiries into the nature of existence.

41. Similarly, much of what Steiner speaks about has import for religion, but is itself not religion, and, therefore, is never demanded to be accepted as a matter of belief.

42. Those who do take up any of Steiner's statements do so, if in the spirit of anthroposophy, either as "indications" worthy of being explored as promising or as findings of which they are convinced on the basis of their own determinations.

43. It is the case that a movement for religious renewal did grow out of Steiner's work. The Christian Community is a religious movement with all of the accouterments and characteristics associated traditionally with religion, and, in this case specifically, Christian religion. It is, however, entirely separate from the Anthroposophical Society in organization and practice. Although the Christian Community draws upon anthroposophy for insight—in a way very similar to that in which Protestant and Catholic process theologians draw upon the process philosophy of Alfred North Whitehead—none of the creeds or practices of the Christian Community are a part of anthroposophy. Rudolf Steiner himself insisted that the Christian Community and the Anthroposophical Society be kept completely separate. He was adamant, moreover, that the Christian Community not be regarded by anthroposophists or others as the anthroposophical church.

44. The Anthroposophical Society is not a religious group. Rather it is a completely open society.

45. Persons can be members of the Anthroposophical Society regardless of their viewpoints on life. Christian, Jew, Muslim, Buddhist, Hindu, Marxist, atheist—all can become members. Nor do they have to surrender their viewpoint at the door to become members.

46. The Anthroposophical Society does not identify itself as a religious group.

47. Unlike most Christian churches, anthroposophy has no creed or any other form of doctrinal statement to which members must or are expected to subscribe.

48. Anthroposophy has no clergy or form of clergy, unlike religious groups, such as the Christian, Jewish, Islamic, and others.

49. Membership in the Anthroposophical Society does not qualify a person to perform a marriage ceremony in New York State.

50. Anthroposophy does not have sacraments, such as the Eucharist and baptism common in most Christian churches.

51. Unlike nearly all religions, such as Christianity, Judaism, Islam, and even some eastern religions, anthroposophy does not claim a sacred scripture unique to itself.

52. Unlike many religions, such as the Catholic Church, most Protestant churches, and Islam, anthroposophy does not have or administer a system of canon law.

53. Anthroposophy does not have ceremonial functions, nor does it hold formal worship services.

54. Anthroposophy does not make efforts at propagation or missionizing, as is often a central activity of many churches and religions.

55. To reiterate, anthroposophy is a way of knowing, a method of inquiry.

56. An atheist may become a member of an anthroposophical society, and remain an atheist; an agnostic may become a member of an anthroposophical society, and remain an agnostic; a member of a traditional religious sect or denomination may become a member of an anthroposophical society, and remain a member of their sect or denomination.

57. In every fundamental respect, anthroposophy is not a religion and the Anthroposophical Society is not a religious organization.

Contributors

Douglas Gerwin, **Ph.D.,** Director of the Center for Anthroposophy and Co-Director of the Research Institute for Waldorf Education, has taught for over 25 years at university and at Waldorf high schools in subjects ranging from biology and history to German and music. A Waldorf graduate, he has edited three books related to Waldorf education — *For the Love of Literature: A Celebration of Language and Imagination; Genesis of a Waldorf High School;* and *The Andover Proceedings: Tapping the Wellsprings of Health in Adolescence* — as well as writing articles on adolescence and the Waldorf curriculum. He is a member of the Pedagogical Section Council and the Leadership Council of the Association of Waldorf Schools of North America.

Douglas Sloan, **Ph.D.,** Professor of History and Education Emeritus at Teachers College, Columbia University, was also coordinator of the religion and education program offered by Teachers College in cooperation with Union Theological Seminary and The Jewish Theological Seminary. From 1992-2000 he was Director of the Masters Program in Waldorf Education at Sunbridge College, where he co-directed the Research Institute for Waldorf Education and served as editor of its *Research Bulletin.* Among his books are *Insight-Imagination: The Emancipation of Thought and the Modern World* and *Faith and Knowledge: Mainline Protestantism and American Higher Education.*

Betty Staley, **M.A.,** Director of Waldorf High School Teacher Education and founding member of Rudolf Steiner College, has been a Waldorf teacher for over 40 years, ranging from early childhood through elementary to the high school grades. She is founder of the Sacramento Waldorf High School, where she has taught English and History for over 25 years. A specialist in adolescent development, her publications include *Between Form and Freedom: A Practical Guide to the Teenage Years; Tapestries: Weaving Life's*

Journey; Soul Weaving; Hear the Voice of the Griot: A Celebration of African Geography, History, and Culture; and most recently, *Adolescence: The Sacred Passage*. She is a member of the Pedagogical Section Council.

Roberto Trostli, M.A., has been active in Waldorf education for over 25 years as a class teacher, high school teacher, adult educator, lecturer, and workshop leader. He has taught at Rudolf Steiner School in New York, NY, Hartsbrook School in Hadley, MA, where he founded its new high school, and Sunbridge College in Spring Valley, NY. The author of *Physics is Fun: A Sourcebook for Teachers* as well as a dozen plays for children, Roberto has also written many articles on Waldorf education and edited *Rhythms of Learning* and *Teaching Language Arts in the Waldorf Schools*. He is a member of the Pedagogical Section Council.

Dorit Winter, M.A., Director of the Bay Area Center for Waldorf Teacher Training as well as founder and coordinator of the Santa Cruz Arts Festival, has been a Waldorf class teacher, German teacher, high school teacher, and adult educator, including 12 years as Director of the San Francisco Waldorf Teacher Training of Rudolf Steiner College. Herself a Waldorf graduate, she is a writer, translator, painter, and flutist. Author of *Because of Yolande, The Art and Science of Teaching Composition*, and *Sheets of Light*, she has written widely on Waldorf education and other anthroposophical subjects.